Laundromats

How to Start, Run & Grow a Successful Washateria Business

By

Rebecca Wilson

Copyright © 2018 – **CSBA Publishing House**

All Rights Reserved.

No part of this publication may be reproduced, stored in a retrieval system or transmitted in any form or by any means, electronic, mechanical, photocopying, recording or otherwise without the proper written consent of the copyright holder, except brief quotations used in a review.

Published by:

CSBA Publishing

CSBA Publishing House

Cover & Interior designed

By

Heather Ross

First Edition

TABLE OF CONTENTS

Preface – My Story 7
History of Laundromat Business 21
Introduction 43
Why Start a Laundromat Business 45
Buying an Existing one Vs. Building a New one 49
    Common Mistakes to Avoid 50
    The Complexity of Running a Laundromat Business ..51
    Due Diligence 52
    Location Analysis 53
    Why is location so important? 54
        Indoor lighting 55
        Outdoor lighting 56
        Cleanliness 57
        Restrooms 58
        Clutter-Free checkout stand/counter 58
        Parking Lot 59
        Ambience 59
        Proper Signage 61
        Operating Hours 61
    Demographics 62
        5 Must Have's For your Laundromat Location 62
    Income Analysis of an existing Laundromat 63
    Expense Analysis 64
    Equipment Analysis 64
    Store Value Analysis 65

SWOT Analysis 66
15 Step Laundromat buying Checklist 69
Where to Find a laundromat to Buy or Lease? 71
    5 Offline Ways to Find a Business for Sale 72
    5 Online Ways to Find a Business for Sale 73
Start-Up Cost For Building a Laundromat 79
    Do Not Do It Alone 80
    Estimated Cost to Open One 81
    Expenses to Build a Laundromat 82
    Estimated Cost of Opening a Laundromat in a Small to Mid-size City 85
    Estimated Monthly Expenses 86
    Estimated Monthly Income Calculation 87
Five Things to Check Out Before Starting a Laundromat Business 91
    Check the Lease of the Laundromat Business 92
    Water Use and Management 93
    Location 94
    Equipment 96
    Competition 99
    Additional Revenue Streams 100
7 most important factors to consider when leasing a facility 102
    Demographic 102
    Accessibility 104
    Building infrastructure 105
    Terms of the lease 106
    Length of the lease 107

- Security deposit 108
- Negotiating the Laundromat Lease 108
- How to Finance a Laundromat Business 111
  - Owner/Seller Financing 112
  - Home Equity Line of Credit (HELOC) 112
  - Small Business Administration Loans (SBA) 113
  - Other Financing Options 114
    - Documents you will need from the Seller 123
    - Documents you will need for Loan application ... 123
- Planning & Build-Out 128
  - Planning Stage 128
  - Build-out 131
- Buying Laundromat Equipment for Your Laundromat Business 134
  - How & Where to Find good used Equipment 138
- Permits & Business Licenses (Uncle Sam) 140
  - Name Your Business 140
  - Incorporating Your Business 142
  - Legal Business Structure 143
    - Sole Proprietor 144
    - Partnership 144
    - Corporation (Inc. or Ltd.) 145
    - S Corporation 146
    - Limited Liability Company (LLC) 147
  - Apply and obtain your Employer Identification number from IRS 148
  - Opening a Commercial Bank Account 150
  - City & County Licenses 151

Three Ways to Increase Your Customer Flow 153
  Upgraded Equipment 154
  Adding Technology 154
  Adding Amenities 155
Laundromat Business Marketing Strategies 157
  Determining Your Audience 157
  Advertise Your Services 158
  Marketing Distribution 159
Top Three Ways to Market Your Laundromat Business 161
  Exterior Signs 162
  Local Area/Store Marketing (LAM/LSM) 162
    Giving Back to the Community 163
Last Words 165
Resources for Laundromat Business 166

PREFACE – MY STORY

My first memories of Laundromats are from when I was young. We had a washer and clothes dryer in our house, but one winter day, one of them, or both, broke. Since they were in our dark, musty basement that had cobwebs in it, I rarely went down there except to shift laundry to the clothes dryer; take clothes out of the dryer and dump them into a basket. Grabbing the pair of jeans I needed; overstuff the washer and start the cycle; or toss lone socks that did not have matches into the, what we called, "sock basket."

The sock basket was giant, capital G, and held, literally, hundreds of loose and lone socks nobody bothered to match and that I bet half of were probably real "loners," in that their matching socks were long gone. Since we had no idea where they went, I imagined them sucked up by the dryer, only to be dropped off in "sock heaven," or worse, dropped on some cold, rainy, dark moor of "sock purgatory." Match-able socks were doomed to be ignored.

The summer before the present winter, my mother and father had divorced, and my dad had taken off for Sarasota, Florida, where he thought he might have potential work, and as a sufferer of Seasonal Affective Disorder (S.A.D.). It was probably a good thing he decided to live there because of the needed sun, blue skies, negative ions, and the warmth. And I do not remember my father being particularly handy except with his guns (only for hunting), his Army jeep, cooking hor'dourves, getting people's cars that were stuck in the snow out in the front of our house out, and the lawn mower.

Our mother had gotten our aging house with its accumulating problems so that with the house came much upkeep along with the eventual breakdowns — the furnace, the mower, the plumbing, you know, stuff like that.

I remember one time trying to install insulation in the garage with my mom, but not as you would think. We did our best, but it was patchwork and only that which we could reach from the cold cement floor of our garage or the rickety wooden stairs from it that lead to the first floor of our aging house (the garage was underground). Besides the task being difficult, the garage was dusty, gray, crumbling, and, in our kid minds, scary, especially with the large gaping hole in the wall near the rickety stairs.

An opening toward a "room" with a low ceiling and dirt floor where old boards from the original building of the house and maybe some trash and other items owned by the builders were thrown in. As kids, of course, we thought of the "room" as a playground for ghosts, witches, vampires, werewolves, and other scary beings (nowhere near as friendly as Casper), let alone mice and possibly other rodents. All that besides kid scary seemed to us as mother scary "entities" too, and we were very protective over our mother, especially considering what she had been through.

But I am not saying we would make sure she got out of the garage first if something terrifying appeared. We were kids first of all ha ha! Anyway, with problems like upkeep and repair, we did our best with our mother bravely always taking the lead.

With little to no money to boot, it was difficult. I do not know how our mother made it through when she mostly had to fend off the bill collectors (with the house Mom, too, got all of our debt and a bankruptcy to boot) and the bills for our braces, our shoes, our coats, our school supplies, our musical instruments, our school club fees, and, etc. (she was not about to make us give up the school activities we loved), and food for three growing and always very hungry kids.

But there were a few of those bill collectors or business owners who were kind to us, especially our pediatrician or the business owners we knew, like the guy who sold Christmas trees. But of those "collectors" who did not get it, life, us, I could not help but think and compare them to Mr. Potter, the money mongering villain, in *it's a Wonderful Life.* Yes, *that* villain.

I will never forget the ones who were kind though, owners of familiar, time trusted, old businesses we frequented (and usually got a piece of candy given to us, my sister, brother, and me!), as did our grandparents, extended family, and dear friends. After all, our family name was known in that town;

we had lived in the city since its beginning, that is, our family had been around a long time, and *would be* around for the duration, a "long time," as we had claimed this theme to bolster ourselves.

In other words, our roots were there, and our roots had been firmly planted, especially, for example, because our great grandfather was one of the seven founders of this somewhat, if not huge, large city. Or anyway, another way to put it is he was up high on the totem pole. And especially because it was familiar so that despite "going poor," as my daughter so innocently but aptly puts it, our mother, and consequently the rest of us, bore the shame of a, if not a contentious divorce, a divorce, all the same; financial problems; a crumbling house; the pattern of wearing the same clothes day after day; and the tarnishing of the family name.

Still, those who looked away to protect us, acting like they did not know, or welcomed us, despite our circumstances, I remember best and with tremendous gratitude and warmth.

In those days the handling of money was so much simpler, at least this is how I remember it, and those like-minded and kind, the George Bailey's, Mary Hatcher's, and even "Angels" like the fumbling but loveable Clarence Odbody, characters in *It's a Wonderful Life,* we knew best, those who would not ever think of sending back nasty red-inked notes on our bills. The others were only red words scrawled across bills, invisible monsters that only visited us in nightmares and taunting dreams, to us.

So the simplicity of not being accosted through the internet or not being assaulted by terrifying threats by bill collectors from other unknown and huge cities far away did not totally scare us but warned us of a different and more complex world coming and at a rapid speed. Still, it was somewhat easier from a landlocked midwestern city town half on Laura Ingalls Wilder's Great Plains (see *On the Banks of Plum Creek)*, in that we were a little bit secluded.

And those crying foul, cold, disgruntled owners of the businesses, the Ebenezer Scrooge's, that plagued us, eventually learned to take what they could get, month to month, and move on with their lacks of kindnesses, their lives. So it was not a surprise when the washer and clothes dryer broke, after preceding breakdowns and other difficulties, and with three "girls'" (my mom, me and my sister, as our brother could have cared less), clothes, even in that day and age (I am trying not to be sexist), especially for teenagers, girls, were of the utmost importance to us. Our mother made due but still managed to look well dressed.

We were lucky. She had style and could create a lot from a little or beauty from the tossed aside, the worn.

So "down" to the Laundromat we went. Our particular Laundromat was deep in the large or small "city," really a town (really, it depended on how you looked at it), but certainly, to us, living by the Country Club out of the city bounds (is that not ironic?), a trek.

However, when we got there or maybe they, my mother, sister, and brother, had just left without me when I was still asleep, my sister was the one who got to stay and do the laundry. I was furious. She got to watch cable in the Laundromat, use the change machine, buy snacks and, best of all, the watching of cable (we were too out of bounds, lived to "far out" of the "city" for cable to reach) where our favorite show, *The Munsters*, was available! And, boy, I can assure you it was on at the Laundromat!

I was still furious when Mom took us, my brother, bored with the thought, and me, "down" to see our sister at the Laundromat later, when I woke up probably, and when we got there, I begged to stay at the Laundromat alone or with my sister. The place was warm from the dryers, not cold like our drafty house, or in a cobwebby basement, there were a lot of windows that caught the light of the sky, despite it being another dreary winter day, so that my sister was having fun being, as usual, the independent leader that she was, in charge.

Plus people smiled at us because we were young and responsibly washing the family's clothes, drying them, and folding them, the clean clothes, that is, doing a supposed adult only chore all by ourselves. So far our laundry, because of my responsible and always supportive and cheerful sister, was washed and dried beautifully, folded and clean, and especially the whites, which were the most tricky to keep bright, because the clean white clothes came from good washers and clothes dryers that were thoroughly maintained.

And people were kindly trading off and sharing those "baskets on wheels," as we referred to them, to transport your laundry to or away from the washers and clothes dryers or, laughingly, putting their kids into the empty "baskets on wheels" for fun, if slow and careful, ride. (Probably you should "not try this at home" though!)

Plus, there was this feeling of camaraderie. Whether you were there because you did not have a washer and clothes dryer, or one or the other, you were a college student, or your clothes dryer or washer or both had broken, the need was the same.

The attendant woman behind the counter, keeping an eye out for problems and fixing those problems, like a broken change machine (or one that needed to be filled!) or the broken machine that held the small cardboard boxes of powdered laundry detergent, just enough to do a load or two of wash, you could buy, or doing laundry herself -- back then there was a service where you could pay for your laundry to be washed, dried, and folded -- a service that was considered a good one, where the clothes were not ironed, but, still, done beautifully — would smile at us encouragingly while doing this laundry that had been dropped off, that is, keeping up with, what was called, the wash – dry – fold service.

But once again, being the middle child, and cranky, fidgety, and somewhat selfish to boot, I had to get back in the car with my brother and mother and go back to what I considered our drafty and cable lacking home that had small windows on that dreary winter day, leaving my more efficient and responsible and cheerful older sister to do her best (which she always did) and finish the job.

It was not until college that I did not have a washer and dryer again. But in the college dorms you could use those washers and clothes dryers provided in the basement, but coming from the sixth floor, where my dorm room was located, when I was afraid of elevators (and percolating in the "un" air conditioned high rise made of cement blocks that sucked in the heat) the Midwestern and plains heat made this an awfully time consuming and hideous job, except that I got a lot of exercise running, or climbing, out of breath, those ugly, hard, dirty, cement stairs that had caused many an ankle to "turn" or sprain, sprain being that it is the more conclusive or a much better word for what usually happened when you ran *down* those stairs.

Plus most college students did not want to wait in the gloomy basement for their laundry to be "done" so they could drag it back up to their dorm rooms to "fold" because they did not want to fold it there (who would?). And the majority of college students often left once dumping their clothes into the washer or stuffing as much clothing they could get into the washer, plunking in their quarters and starting the washer's cycle and did not come back for hours.

Their clothes left done and wet in the washer, or done and waiting in the clothes dryer, risked other college students stealing their clothes or, irritated, pulling out your stuff, long done, from the washer and tossing it aside on whatever chipped counter that was usually dirty. Or if your stuff was in the clothes dryer, and after one quarter if you were lucky and had quarters. Because there was no change machine or it was broken, not done, still damp, the annoyed college student who did not bother waiting for you to retrieve your stuff would toss the damp clothes on a dusty table, half ruining what the washer had done. Or, even if your clothes were dry, but you had abandoned them, the college student would again pull your stuff out of the clothes dryer and toss it aside in the dust.

Apparently, those college laundry memories are not as comforting as the ones I had of our town Laundromat when I was young and come from dealing with anything other than a real Laundromat. So to reminisce and think about what I, and possibly and hopefully and especially even you, know about true Laundromats, even the more complicated memories of them, say, in a city, but still ultimately with the warmth and ease of them that has been portrayed here, the lack of complexity, not a lot of complicated equipment, but the simple machines on the periphery, top loaders, front loaders, all; a change maker; most likely a TV on the wall; "wheeling baskets"; and the tables and chairs that were perpetually clean and upright, perhaps is inspiring.

Go into a Laundromat. It is almost, because of no need to change it, except for upgrades here and there of the washers and dryers, a fancier TV, the way it should be, wonderfully easy, and almost the same.

Hopefully this preface, my words, will invite you to go on to read the rest of the book and decide if this option of starting a laundry business should be more than an idea or more than causing you to remember or more than causing you to enjoyably remember or more than causing you to joyfully experience (or not!) my memory and a business you can have or run or build or lease for the long term and maybe even pass down to your kids or eventually open more, two, three, four, five, even six!

See if it is feasible by reading the following pages and, at the least -- I find these informational books about how to open various businesses are full of thought-provoking facts, or at the very least contain excellent tips, information that applies to all businesses -- you will learn about starting a business in general and continue on your quest, perhaps, of finding a business or businesses that you will own, lease and/or build, only to prosper and one(s) that are just right for you.

Think about it. It is pretty much a basic human right — to have clean clothes. Everyone needs clean clothes. And that is business security. The need will never go away.

HISTORY OF LAUNDROMAT BUSINESS

It is difficult to build, lease, and/ or own a Laundromat without knowing its history, the foundation, from which you will make decisions. I find it also creates a wisdom in the owner that inspires her to be a part of that history, and by seeing the changes and inventions that came before, over the years, one can, I find, be available or open to new insights and new ideas to come in, making the Laundromat, theirs, better, a niche, a focus, exciting, and fun, so that one's instinct for the business is primed and will add to the long, wonderful, exciting American history of the business.

Think "retro" or "vintage" as possibilities, for example, as clientele change, grow, and/ or get more wonderfully diverse. Inspiration and hope and joy are everything. You must take on or build or own what you love or are excited about.

So it will benefit you to know the original washing machine, a rotary one*, was created by a man named Hamilton Smith. The original washing machine invented specifically for the home was created and introduced by William Blackstone, a citizen of Indiana, in 1874. Fun fact: He built this early washer for his wife as a birthday present! Yet owning one was a luxury most could not afford.

Luckily, J.F. Cantrel, after having taken stock of his community in Fort Worth, Texas, realized that setting up four washing machines and four clothes dryers in a building for citizens without to use with only a small amount of change, even with paying by the hour which was how it was done, might be a necessity and a chore taken care of for some and simply less work, more ease, for others.

So it will also benefit you to know that the first public Laundromat, initially called a "Wash-a-teria," opened on April 14, 1934, in Fort Worth, Texas, according to the Census Bureau. The opening was not happenstance. The new self-service industry, from such things as gas stations to grocery stores, became popular because of its less cost for customers being a prime need during the Depression Era. But also know, that name, "Wash-a-teria," could be switched out with the synonyms, launderette, launderettes, and Washateria, depending on where you lived, your part of the country, as in these names were determined by your region.

And new owners mostly copied the original Wash-a-terias which meant they were not "exclusively coin-operated," but did not "always have an attendant on duty." It was not for three more years that the fully automatic washing machine was invented, paving the way for the first totally unattended Laundromat, paving the way again for the first totally unattended

Laundromat that was open 24 hours a day that Laundromat having opened in the late 1940s.

Previous to all this, Laundromats, now completely self-service focused, were not the Laundromats we now know at all but businesses, sometimes home businesses, that offered laundering and folding, this being known and sometimes, but rarely, *is* known as the wash – dry - fold service. Pressed clothing for their customers being a whole other thing. Until some of them started adding dry cleaners to their Laundromats.

As things progressed, in the 1950s, after the spread of self-service Laundromats opening occurred during the Depression Era, the number of openings picked up again because of the populations of cities heightening. Also in the 50s, and then 60s and 70s, owners started investing in janitorial services to maintain their Laundromats and started investing in equipment, maintenance, and even dry cleaner services within the Laundromat for those who wanted them.

In the present, you can find the owners of Laundromats have kept up with new inventions. The machines are more energy efficient, while low water washers and dryers that are able to dry more clothes much faster are taking on importance. And, yes, there are still coin-operated machines but also digital card operated systems are available. Laundromats are also answering new demands by making Wi-Fi available and, of course, TV's, even Flat Screen TV's, and vending machines, sometimes even arcade games available.

And imagine, even, how those vending machines have changed, often providing healthier snacks, even organic snacks — let alone how the TV has advanced to having an array of possibilities to heighten your experience while watching the Flat Screen. Often you will even find children's play areas within the Laundromat, like those you can find almost everywhere now, even, now, in airports.

In the end, we can conclude that Laundromats, the way they are termed now, have appealed to people and do now because of need, necessity, and economy. And we have not even talked about the social aspect of the Laundromat clearly explored in movies, songs, and novels.

Those, too, in the cities of consumers frequenting "their" Laundromats that had quickly become a meeting place, a hubbub, on Friday and Saturday nights, to catch up, gossip, socialize, and debate while their children gathered and played and *while* they took care of the chore, washing and drying their clothes, that felt lessened by the Laundromat experience! Think of how many friendships were made there, romances blossomed there, and business partners found each other there — because of all these reasons and more.

Finally, let us remember there is such a thing as gender technology. We know clothes, before anything taken up and described here, were cleaned along rivers with rocks used to beat the clothes clean and in descriptions and pictures we see women taking on this chore. And we have not even addressed washboards.

As discussed, the washer has come a long way, but because the chore was seemingly more often designated as the woman's chore and with that "understanding" came the "washer woman" for the wealthy so that the wealthy depended on these businesses to take care of their dirty laundry and likewise the washer woman with her home business depending on those wanting their laundry done for them as their economic means.

Given the history, with the designated washerwomen, it is not odd that early advertisements concerning all things washer and laundry were geared toward women primarily using such things as boiling water and scrub boards.

*This washer was operated by a crank that had to be turned by hand to make a perforated cylinder inside another cylinder rotate whereby it turned on an axis. The two cylinders operated by one being wooden and the other being metal and one of the cylinders inside the other cylinder, the other cylinder wrapping it, the perforations in one cylinder allowing water to be forced through the clothing inside the inner cylinder.

Now let us look at the invention and history of the clothes dryer!

It is tricky to track a clear path concerning the beginnings of the clothes dryer. "Things" overlap, so out of a fear of leaving out names, dates, variations, and etc., I am going to tell you what is, we know, for sure about the invention process of the clothes dryer.

The clothes dryer, or clothes ventilator as it was first referred to, first showed up in the late 1800s in England, France, and the United States. And, who knows, at this state and in other states of the invention process of the clothes dryer, the clothes dryer could have been appearing in other countries, other parts of the world, but it is just not on record in a place for us to know for sure.

Early on, the clothes dryer was invented because of exasperation; the fact that hanging one's clothes outside to dry did not always mean your clothes, outside, *would* get dry. In the winter, at least on a cold enough day in winter, to be frank, your clothes basically froze.

In the rain, because you had hung out your clothes to dry thinking it was going to be a nice enough day and then left for duties or errands or work, your clothes obviously got wetter, or your clothes stayed wet and/, or your clothes got cold(er) and wet(ter) and then your clothes most likely had to be washed all over again because of each scenario, let alone thawed out if it happened to be a or turn into a cold winter day.

So it seems a natural response for humans to start looking for ways to speed up the process of getting their clothes to dry and make easier the process of getting their clothes to dry. Regardless, as often as it is with beginnings, we were on extremely, even if hopeful, shaky ground, in that sometimes things get messier before they get better. There was the idea of building a "clothes dryer shed," putting a stove in it, and hanging one's clothes in the shed so that they could dry — at least on rainy days or on a cold day in winter.

Then came along the "drum" idea. Whereby you put your wet clothes in a drum, the drum having smallish holes in it, and turned the drum with a crank, that is, *you* turned the drum with the crank, as in the "drum turning" was human powered. The drum would have been placed near a fire that would dry the clothes somewhat evenly.

The problem was your clothes would come out smoky, and your clothes would come out with a dusting of soot and sometimes, maybe even if only partially, your clothes would come out burned and that is in the best case scenario.

I mean that hopefully your clothes had not caught completely on fire and been destroyed. At this point, one wonders if this process, while a little more manageable in terms of weather, really took much less time and was worth it, given that you might have to replace some of your clothes or all of your clothes.

Eventually, even though it took a while because of things like money, human interest and determination and stamina and being in for the long haul, sourcing, the rocky road of patents, sponsoring companies, and etc., we got to what we all think of, basically, as a clothes dryer's clothes dryer, a machine with a drum that turns because of electricity and is heated by electricity.

As my husband says, basically a simple machine, the clothes dryer. Still, the high price tag of the clothes dryer meant that it pretty much was out of reach for all but the wealthy. Yet with more fine-tuning, the clothes dryer became more accessible for the middle class and, perhaps, lower classes, to buy and more inexpensive for those of the middle class to buy and, perhaps, those of the lower classes to possibly buy.

Still, it wasn't until the 40s that the surge of clothes dryer buying took off even more because competitors selling the clothes dryers had to beat out each other by offering the lowest sale prices of the clothes dryers.

And there were various manufacturers and owners of the clothes dryer businesses that competed to get the attention of the clothes dryer buyers so that they had to advertise that they, the business owners and the manufacturers of the clothes dryers, had the best quality of clothes dryers to buy, or they had to advertise that they, the business owners and manufacturers of the clothes dryers, had the clothes dryers that were the best designed to buy, or the business owners and manufacturers of clothes dryers had to advertise that they had the clothes dryers that were the least expensive to buy, and etc.

This surge meant that the clothes dryer manufacturers such as General Electric and other clothes dryer manufacturers counted on selling a lot of clothes dryers, given, according to the census bureau, that there were already 60,000, this being the number of clothes dryers in homes in the United States, those same clothes dryers being fueled either by gas or electricity.

After World War II ended, it is estimated that only ten percent of our population owned clothes dryers. But with World War II having ended and the Baby Boomers beginning to have their reign with the upward boom in the economy things were changing.

With Whirlpool being the first to claim that their regular speed clothes dryers took only half the time to dry the clothes, in that they manufactured the clothes dryers with an increased airflow and smaller amount of gas needing to be used, the soldiers coming home, the Baby Boomer generation taking the lead, jumped on the opportunity to buy the clothes dryers for their families, given that Whirlpool's advances spread to other clothes dryer companies.

And these new consumers of the clothes dryers were rewarded by further advancements, such as with the newest models and makes of the clothes dryers of the companies making them, the clothes dryers having things like temperature controls, exhaust systems, and even timers to determine the clothes drying duration, that is, new offerings as the advanced systems of the clothes dryers became fine-tuned.

And in many ways, the making of these kinds of clothes dryers and the competitiveness of the business owners of the clothes dryer stores offering them, because the numbers of the clothes dryers, those clothes dryers being bought, to surge even more.

In addition, there now were clothes dryer dryness censors whereby the clothes dryer itself would turn off when it sensed the clothes were dry. This invention saved money for the consumer of the clothes dryers. More improvements in the 40s meant the controls of the clothes dryer were moved to the front of the clothes dryer, a timer was affixed to the clothes dryer, an exhaust system attached for moist air for the clothes dryer, and a cycle just for a "cool-down" period was available on the clothes dryer.

Finally, all said, the clothes dryers, in 1958, started sporting a negative pressure system for the clothes dryer to dry clothes and, remarkably, that negative pressure system for the clothes dryer is still used today. Also, notice that over the years, the clothes dryer, unlike the snack machine, still revolves around the quarter mostly. If you do not believe me, head into your closest Laundromat and gaze.

Next, in the 60s, you got better quality clothes dryer dryness sensors, improvements in time aspects of the clothes dryer, including a more fine-tuned choice for the length of time and dryness levels and even permanent press cycles were added to the clothes dryer.

Following, in 1983 the consumers could actually delay start times of their clothes dryers or have the clothes dryer start at specific times of the day that the owner of the clothes dryer had previously "programmed" the clothes dryer to start. This conserving of the energy of the clothes dryer had taken root in the 1980s too, but just before that, in the 70s, electric starters were available on gas dryers, securing for the first time that both resources and "fuels" were taken advantage of in a new and positive way for the clothes dryer.

We know that value of efficiency concerning fuel and the longevity of the environment has held true into the present whereby saving trees to saving fuel to saving the ozone layer or endangered animals by not using aerosols and to buying fuel efficient and hybrid and safe cars is like an ingrained value almost everyone sees as an obligation. And, in fact, this, like the clothes dryer's evolvement, has paved the way for many changes, inventions and the tweaking of products to make them more "healthy" and/ or just plain better for the environment, man and woman kind, our world.

We can, in one way, thank the evolution (among many other things) of the clothes dryer not only to be a part of this history of understanding how to grow, invent and change for the better but also be a part of this change, these changes, that has lead the way.

Finally, in 1968, even a clothes dryer using microwaves was introduced for study by M. Levison, but, as of yet, the scientists called upon to help study the effect and outcomes have been unable to rule out their concerns for the safety of the consumer. Solar clothes dryers that appear to be safer and very good for the environment given the current warnings of our nation using up our part of the planet's fuel and natural resources are also in the works.

Too, now, one can choose between "spin" clothes dryers and "tumble" clothes dryers whereby the energy savings make the spin clothes dryer that leaves your clothes not completely dry but damp is certainly energy efficient. Too there are the Condensing or Vent-less Clothes Dryers where both the washer and the clothes dryer are on the same machine.

Yet the concern is that only the washer part is more energy efficient while the clothes dryer drying cycle is less energy efficient than those of a "normal" standard in a "regular" clothes dryer. And there is way much more information out there to be explored concerning efficiency and the latest upgrades of clothes dryers.

Finally and wonderfully and wildly positive is that in 1985 the first all-Spanish instructions in manuals (alongside the instructions, etc., in English), instructions on labels, and instructions on consoles of clothes dryers, their controls, were unveiled.

Other improvements were a choice in large type as opposed to small type in manuals and the same choices concerning large type as opposed to small type on labels and even large type as opposed to small type on consoles of clothes dryers.

There, beginning in the 80s, are even clothes dryers that besides having larger type and/ or being in Spanish have graphics or even bigger graphics to help one to see and problem - solve and the bigger controls on the clothes dryers for the same reasons, besides making the clothes dryers easier to hang on to. So that all these possibilities, you can imagine, help non-native speakers of English, in that their first language is Spanish, along with helping the elderly, the poor sighted and those who have arthritis.

In the present we have "green" clothes dryers that focus on even greater fuel economy, energy efficiency, that is, so that less natural resources need to be used to operate the said machine, the clothes dryer, and that the operation of it does not have an output that is bad for the environment.

For example, we now have the Hydronic Clothes Dryer created by Hydromate Technologies which uses hydronic power to dry the clothes, and there are even LED touch screens on the clothes dryers that even I, someone not too hip concerning the updated technologies, have tuned into one of these options.

We are currently renting a place that has one of the latest models of clothes dryers. I had thought this particular clothes dryer would be too complicated for me to handle, that I would always have to have the manual of my clothes dryer on hand and that having to choose from so many options concerning how to dry my clothes would be extremely troublesome. Not so. It is logical.

You do not need a clothes dryer's manual for my particular model. In fact, we found no manual was available for this particular clothes dryer when we moved in. Or at least we could not find one.

But it is simple.

You touch this clothes dryer's power button and the drying options light up. And you just touch the options you want for drying your clothes and Wallah your clothes dryer runs smoothly! Plus, with our model, the "buzzer" that sounds to say your clothes are dry is sing-songy and very pleasant, not at all jarring or annoying, and it, the pleasing song, lasts a long while so that you can be sure to happen upon the sound, say, if you are moving through the different rooms of your apartment, condo, or house. Plus, you can always turn the sound, letting you know that your clothes are dry, down or even off.

My experience is that this was not always an option – turning the, not "song," but buzzer off – on older models or, even, having a buzzer that lets you know that your clothes are dry in the first place to turn off! Still, I prefer the clothes dryer "song" on to tell me, signal to me, my clothes are dry, because I am a little spacy-er than most and will simply forget I have clothes drying in the clothes dryer and be behind on my laundry or let my now dry laundry get especially wrinkled (let alone let my clothes waiting in the washer get mildewy if this goes on for days) before remembering I have clothes in the clothes dryer.

Still, there is always the newly - offered refresh option on my clothes dryer (a digital "button" to push on my clothes dryer) . . . Still, even with this wonderful backup, I have wasted time, so, if *still* home, I love this gentle musical reminder.

Technology updates for things like TV's, phones, washers, clothes dryers and pretty much anything needing, in order to be current, updates beyond the basics and their simple designs have been, for the most part, helpful. And if not "green," manufacturers are working on such because of consumer demand.

Lastly, the icing on the cake, for me at least, is that today your clothes dryer may feature noise reduction and vibration reduction so that your clothes dryer is a quieter clothes dryer, this being needed especially if you live in a condo or apartment (or, even, in my mind, have a sleeping child), improving the quality of washing and drying your clothes one more step.

Another help to maintain this feature to keep your clothes dryer (and washer!) quiet is some clothes dryers now have a *self-adjusting* system in terms of the excessive shaking and/ or the "walking" (where the washer and/ or the clothes dryer moves a little across the floor because of the shaking) of the clothes dryer (and, again, this applies to the washer of course!) that control this excessive shaking in the clothes dryer (and washer!) that, because of having this annoying juggling or "walking," can lead to the clothes dryer's instability.

INTRODUCTION

Given all the back story and history lessons, hopefully, I didn't bore you too much and I am hoping instead you feel you are ready to go in terms of setting up this business, feel you have a thorough foundation and, perhaps, are inspired. I find knowledge is power and allows me to understand my current process better, as explained before so that you are ready to get into the steps of setting up a "Washateria," Launderette, or Laundromat, any of the names that you can choose from, depending on your tastes.

But, as with starting any business, you will have to be "all in," excited, and hopeful. And I am not saying that at times you will not feel overwhelmed or confused or that the path is or will be too arduous, even when starting out, but, as always, it is often a good sign, as in when taking a test. The best state of mind to be in when taking a test is slightly frustrated or nervous. If you are lackadaisical or *completely* lost from beginning to the end of your test, you will not do as well. It is somewhat like the labor of giving birth to a child where sometimes, especially somewhere toward the end, you want to give up, but that point is called, believe it or not, transition.

Transition simply means you are shifting from "doing" to the determination phase. So what I am saying is expect periods of being overwhelmed or something close. You may be "transitioning," getting the "rest" you need, or being honest about your state. It does not mean you are doomed.

It is that you need this place to be in, that it is part of the process, even if it is just being "slightly" frustrated. Like any worthwhile process, from setting up a business to creating a piece of art to taking a test to bringing a child into the world (some people consider their business their child!), it will not be "perfect" or "smooth sailing," but it will likely be worth it.

WHY START A LAUNDROMAT BUSINESS

From a business standpoint, a Laundromat has minimal monthly expenses and often no employees, unless you have an "attendant" who works behind a counter mostly taking on the Wash and Fold part of the business or the light maintenance of your machines, such as filling the change machine with quarters aspect of your business, which is separate from the self-serve aspect whereby customers do their own laundry with the available machines.

Within the Wash and Fold aspect of your business, if you choose to offer one, there is no ironing offered, unlike with the cleaners. Customers simply drop off their laundry, the attendant takes care of it, and the customer picks it up on an agreed upon date or even waits for it, especially if you offer Wi-Fi and other conveniences they can use to work or keep themselves entertained.

Or your Laundromat can be unattended only requiring maintenance and cleaning as you see fit. And only if you are talented in either or both aspects might you want to take on these services yourself instead of hiring someone to do them. I really believe in this.

Hiring someone for things that are not really your specialty or that you have no desire to learn or deal with in that the thought of them or one causes you dread, dread not being the same as a "heightened" sense of anxiety but, well, dread, pretty much a horrific place to be in (see me for an understanding of dread haha) is a *good* thing to do.

For instance, cleaning is my forte. I'm good at it, I need to clean my surroundings to be able to think, and clean space, like a clean Laundromat, invites me in and makes me want to do my laundry there, and even gives me a sense of happiness. So if I owned a Laundromat, I would take this task on.

But given that I am not good at tweaking or problem solving when it comes to machines, I would hire someone to do such. Otherwise it would take me much longer, and I would lose business, I'm sure, in the process. Plus I would dread those days or hours when I would have to take on such. So here, as a reminder, and some general facts for the first time in this book, are the basic facts about the laundry business:

- The laundry industry is about 70 years old, and the business has constantly been growing.
- The United States currently has about 30,000 Laundromats.

- The laundry business is pretty much a recession-proof industry, in that there is always a need for clean clothes, no matter what the state of the economy is in the United States.
- The economic aspect of the United States Laundry Business is that the Laundry Business offers a gross revenue per year of $5 billion.
- The Laundromat owner can have an income that can average between $5,000 and $25,000. If you are wondering how, well that is what we will discuss in this book.

So read on.

BUYING AN EXISTING ONE VS. BUILDING A NEW ONE

A lot of this answer comes down to your experience and expertise in running a business in general – or not having any experience in running a business in general! Also, keep in mind that there may already be laundry businesses in the areas that need them and/ or the areas you are considering. You also want to remember that building a laundry business, any business, from scratch is a very detailed process.

You may or will need to make site improvements, such as upgrading the electrical, plumbing, HVAC and many other similar items of your space. If you are building it on leased space, then yes, you do have to deal with your landlord and get their approval to all the modifications and constructions to their facility. You will also have to learn to navigate the negotiations that come along with leasing.

On the other hand, when you buy an existing Laundromat business, it should come with an existing client base, which can often reduce the risk involved. No matter what route you choose there are four common mistakes you want to avoid.

COMMON MISTAKES TO AVOID

Starting a Laundromat business offers you many advantages. However, there are four common mistakes you need to avoid making. Let's see how you can learn from the mistakes of others and have a strong business.

THE COMPLEXITY OF RUNNING A LAUNDROMAT BUSINESS

Most assume owning a Laundromat business requires nothing more than providing the washers and the dryers. While operating a Laundromat business can be fairly easy, it is more complex than you may think as has been alluded to previously. A Laundromat is still a business like any other and needs to be properly managed in order to be successful.

This means you need to think like a business owner and have an entrepreneurial mindset. As far as the operations of your Laundromat business go, there is more than just overseeing and collecting money. You also need to manage the staff, unless you are the staff, oversee and/ or provide the maintenance, oversee or, on your own, manage the marketing and the advertising, and oversee and/ or manage the bookkeeping.

But even if you are not proficient in these areas and you hire someone to do them you still want a basic understanding of these areas, so you know what to look for and what to ask to be done and those to hire and to know when things are running smoothly – or not.

DUE DILIGENCE

The most important part of buying or building a business is proper research and analysis of the prospect. This is where many do not do their due diligence. Perhaps it is because you are excited and just want to get your Laundromat business up and running or perhaps, even, the research you have done, or you're thinking that you already know what to do causes you to skip this part of setting up your Laundromat business.

But not taking on this process can be self-sabotage. And, yes, this is a very detailed process that may also make you want to avoid it, but, in the end, you must not avoid it, and it should not be rushed.

How do you get through? Have a plan, write it down generally, even if it is what I call a "skeleton" outline if that is all you can do. Let that be good enough. And then each day take up a piece of that plan, just one piece, and flesh it out, still, if need be, "skeleton ish" but a part of the big picture none the less. But do not let anyone talk you into shortchanging your due diligence.

There are five areas of due diligence you need to focus on before buying, leasing or building a Laundromat business.

LOCATION ANALYSIS

There are a few things to consider when it comes to the location of a Laundromat business. You want to check off and analyze the following. And if you do not know what each means in detail, research! Googling is a fine thing! That is why it has become a verb in our language!

- Location Analysis
- Perform a demographic analysis.
- Perform a competition analysis.
- Obtain (and complete, if necessary) any current building plans for your building and any other permits for remodels or new construction in the area.

- Age, brand, and condition of equipment (when buying)
- Recommended upgrades
- Condition of the facility including electrical, plumbing & HVAC (when buying)

Regardless if you are building a new one or buying an existing one, this is the section where you should spend most of your time, effort and energy into at first. If you do these above seven research properly, your success rate will be very high.

Let me quickly address each of these items, so you will understand why I am stressing over these factors so much.

WHY IS LOCATION SO IMPORTANT?

Well, let's see, your business place /location is one of the most important factor is your long-term survival effort, because location can make or break a business, you may have the best product, food, and service but if the facility is not clean, not inviting, not well lit, does not have easy in and out access then chances are that business will fail or not succeed to its full potential.

The reality is when choosing what business you need to buy, first and foremost your attention should be at the facility itself or place and its layout and access, remember there are few things you can change and improve, and there are some things which you can not. For example, if the in and out access is difficult, you can not change that on the other hand if the facility is not well lit or dirty and unclean, you can most likely change that with some minimal effort.

So picking the right location is always the most important key to your success. Having said that now let's take a look a look at a list of things you can do to make your facility stand out in the crowd and improve your sales and grow your business. Some of these items may seem obvious or even silly at first but bear with me as I explain the importance of each of the items in this list.

INDOOR LIGHTING

Is your store well lit?

You can have the best machines, beautiful layout and very clean store but if your store is not well lit, it will not attract customer. It is also a big security risk for your customers at night. A well-lit facility gives the sense of security that most dim lit facilities do not. Most stores are fitted with 48-inch fluorescent light bulbs, and they are easy to replace and do not cost as much.

One point to remember, there are 4 types of bulbs, first you can opt for LED bulbs which will replace the fluorescent ones without changing the whole fixtures, they tend to cost more, rest of the 3 types are your typical fluorescent bulbs, but they come in 3 varieties: cool white 34 watts, warm white 34 watts and daylight 34 watts, you can also find all 3 varieties in 40 watts, I always choose the 40 watts bright white or daylight ones as they make the store very bright and well lit.

OUTDOOR LIGHTING

Is your parking lot well-lit at night?

Proper outdoor lighting is very important for your store's security and business. Many studies shows women tend to avoid poorly lit stores at night for obvious security reasons. So pay attention to that, if you have blown parking lot lights, replace them, if you have some pole or area lights out replace them as well.

If your store is an older facility one easy way to add area light is installing some wall mounted an outdoor light on the building focusing on the parking lot. Lately, there are many LED conversion kits are being sold for a reasonable price, and they can reduce your power bill by about 30%.

CLEANLINESS

Is your store clean?

Typically laundromats are high traffic locations, so it is hard to keep them clean, but taking a few steps to make them appear clean is the key. Make sure no loose paper or visible dirt or sand on the floor, no water spill is on the floor. Then look at your washers and dryers especially the ones that are close to the front door as those doors open and close more than 100 times a day, so the dust settles easily on those machines faster. Assign your night shift employee to dust and wipe each and every machine and all the countertops every night or whenever your store is slow.

RESTROOMS

Are your restrooms clean?

Depending on your location and size of the business chances are your restrooms stay busy. It is one of the hardest things to maintain in our business, but it has to be done. Train every employee to go and check restroom every hour, make sure it is stocked with both paper towels and toilet paper, and that it is clean, it has soaps, and the floor is not wet. Also, a good idea to add an automatic air freshener in each toilet to make them smell good.

CLUTTER-FREE CHECKOUT STAND/COUNTER

Is your checkout stand full of shelves and products?

If you are looking to buy a multi-revenue laundromat where they offer wash and fold, snack and beverage bar and other novelty items for sale, then pay attention and see if the shelves, countertops and checkout stand are clean and clutter free or not.

PARKING LOT

Is your parking lot clean?

The first impression is always the most important one. When people drive up to your store, the first thing they see is your parking lot and parking spaces, and if your parking lot is full of debris, empty soda cans, and cigarette buds all over, then you just lost the chance to create an excellent first impression. A good habit would be to schedule and train your employees to go out to the parking lot twice a day and pick up all trash and debris.

AMBIENCE

How do your store smell and feel?

Thinking why am I asking this odd question? Well to a few well-known researchers the smell and feel of a retail store can boost or lose sales, and it is true.

Walk into any big box retail store, you will notice the smell is fresh and inviting, the air temp is not too cool not too warm, and there is music playing in the background. I recently tested this in one of my stores where I added some music by adding an old receiver I had laying around the house and added two ceiling mount speakers which cost around 100 bucks.

I also added a few automatic air freshener that sprays every few minutes in and around the store, especially around the entrance. Right after I did these, I started hearing compliments as to how nice and clean the store is and in 3 months I noticed my snack and drink sales have increased by about 15%! People associate the good smell with a clean environment and thus think the snack or service we sell are better quality.

PROPER SIGNAGE

Do you have proper and adequate signage in your store?

For example, do your customers always walk and ask where the restroom is or where the change machine is?? if, so that is an indication that you do not have properly placed signs in your store. You also need to make sure you place a sign where you explain all your pricing for all washers and dryers by size. If you offer wash and fold service, have a separate sign for that along with $ price per pound.

OPERATING HOURS

Do you have proper hours of operation?

Most neighborhood Washateria typically open around 6 in the morning and close around 10 at night, but how do you know if that your optimal business hours? Do you adjust your hours for the summer months vs. the winter? Finding out the best opening hours for your business actually may increase your sales by a double-digit sometimes.

DEMOGRAPHICS

Demographics is essentially the key to your success or failure. So it is vital that you pay attention. A driving factor in the success of your laundromat business will be location, location, location. Your laundromat business must be located in a prime location spot to be extremely business advantageous and to make the most of the nearby customer demographic, i.e., the people in your neighborhood.

5 MUST HAVE'S FOR YOUR LAUNDROMAT LOCATION

The best location should have these followings:

- Moderate foot traffic
- Mid to low-income housing
- Median income level less than $40K/year
- Blue collar neighborhood
- Mixed race neighborhood

Is the location spot that you are considering for your laundromat business site already saturated with other laundromat businesses in the area? Then why would you build there?

Also, you will give your direct competition every reason to pull every promotional strategy that they have to try to put you out of business since they would have been in the area longer than you. You need to have a laundromat location that is readily accessible to your customer demographic but one that is also strategically distant from your direct, and indirect if possible, competitors as much as possible.

INCOME ANALYSIS OF AN EXISTING LAUNDROMAT

A critical part of buying a Laundromat is to verify the reported income. At a minimum, you want to do an income analysis, verify the bank statements for deposits, examine sales receipts, monitor store collections and take water meter readings. You can also monitor traffic on a given week and see how many customers are coming and out.

EXPENSE ANALYSIS

In this step, you want to account for each and every expense associated with the Laundromat business operation. Some common expenses that get missed include the following:

- Payroll
- Workers compensation
- Repairs and maintenance
- Personal property tax
- Business tax
- Triple net expenses
- Cleaning supplies
- Security system fees

EQUIPMENT ANALYSIS

You should get a list of service items by having a mechanic test all machines. Ask for the maintenance repair schedule, the past repair receipts, and the age and model of all the machines. Acquire any of the manuals of the different models of the washers and the clothes dryers and any other machines in you laundry business, such as the change machine.

If they have been lost, for instance, there is a possibility they are online, or you can find them on eBay and/ or other sites that are similar to eBay. Next, check for any leaks or pipe corrosion. Inspect the electrical for any code violations and that all machines are equipped with an emergency shut off switches.

STORE VALUE ANALYSIS

A Laundromat's value is often based upon a multiple called the Store Value Multiplier or SVM of its monthly net income. The SVM starts at 50 and is adjusted up or down based on the following:

- The lease
- The equipment
- The competition
- The Local Market Conditions (LMC);
- and anything else that requires your attention:
- Other factors

Most Store Value Multipliers (SVM's) are between 45 and 65. For example, if the monthly net income of a

Laundromat business were $4,000, then the worth would be between $180,000 and $260,000.

SWOT ANALYSIS

SWOT (Strength, Weakness, Opportunities & Threat) is a very self-explanatory tool, take a look and see if you can place each of the proposed locations in these quadrants.

Strengths (internal, positive factors) Strengths describe the positive attributes, tangible and intangible, of your organization. These are within your control.	**Weaknesses** (internal, negative factors) Weaknesses are aspects of your business that detract from the value you offer or place you at a competitive disadvantage
Opportunities (external, positive factors) Opportunities are external attractive factors that represent reasons for your business to exist and prosper	**Threats** (external, negative factors) Threats are external factors beyond your control that could put your business at risk. You may benefit from having contingency plans for them.

Once you know the ideal location, time to start negotiating your lease. A commercial lease is very different than most residential leases. Most commercial leases are often quoted as per square feet in dollar amount which typically doesn't include CAM (Common Area Maintenance). You have to add both costs then multiply that number with your exact leased square footage to know what you will be paying.

Did you know that a commercial lease can have a clause where the landlord can get you out of business in just 30 days? How about the other clause where they can walk-in to your premises even when you are closed, and no one is at your location? Well, this is true, they can so it is always a good idea to have your lease reviewed by an attorney, so you know what is in that lease.

It is also a good idea to negotiate an exit strategy at least for the first year, so in the event, if your business doesn't flourish as you imagine, you can get out within the first year without having to pay any more penalties or other fees.

15 Step Laundromat buying Checklist

Here is a general checklist when you are buying a laundromat.

1. Inspection of the equipment

2. Valuation of the business

3, Letter of Intent to the seller

4. Hire a commercial appraiser for an appraisal

5. Price negotiation

6. Signing a purchase agreement

7. Loan application (if you need a bank loan)

8. File your corporation

9. Apply for EIN number

10. Setting up the closing date

11. Setting up Business Bank Account

12. Setting up Payroll service

13. Applying for Business License

14. Meet the employees

15. The Actual closing

WHERE TO FIND A LAUNDROMAT TO BUY OR LEASE?

If you are new to laundromat business but have enough interest to dig deeper, then the next step for you is to try and find a few businesses for sale and evaluate them the best way possible and see if any of them fit your budget and needs.

Laundromat is truly a recession-proof business and still provides a comfortable living for a family. Not to mention the freedom it provides by having and owning your own business.

If you are serious about finding a suitable laundromat business to buy or lease, there are many ways to find a few that are for sale in your area.

You can try both Online and Offline ways.

5 OFFLINE WAYS TO FIND A BUSINESS FOR SALE

- Through Local business brokers (Some national and some local. Two of the major national brokerage companies are Sunbelt and Nationwide business brokers. Local or statewide)
- Through Local commercial real estate agents
- Through Local newspaper classified
- Through Local or national trade show offerings
- Through Vendors (this works better if you are already in this line of business)

5 ONLINE WAYS TO FIND A BUSINESS FOR SALE

There are some very reputable websites you can go and check for sale listings; then there are also online auction houses that sell laundromats among other businesses.

1. First, check out bizbuysell.com. This site is similar to realtor.com for home real estate, but in this site, business brokers list their businesses that are for sale.

2. Try searching on NRC.com and Loopnet.com. Both of these are big players when it comes to the online business brokerage. You will find both "for sale stores" and "for Lease stores."

3. Craigslist ads. Yes, you can find them under "business for sale."

4. Do a search on Coin Laundry Association "For Sale" page at

http://www.coinlaundry.org/investor-resources/businesses-for-sale

5. You can also just do a google search by typing "laundromat for sale in Los Angeles, Ca" Just mention your city and state and see what comes up.

But before you contact any of the sellers or brokers, you need to have your game plan set, so you don't sound like you are just browsing the market.

Business brokers are very different than typical home real estate agents. If a broker senses that you are not serious, they may not even disclose some of their prime listings to you. The reason is simple; they don't want to take a buyer who is not serious to a seller who is motivated to sell. This can take away from the broker's credibility in front of the seller. Also, sellers typically only want serious and qualified buyers that are ready to buy.

You will notice that, before a broker discloses any information about a business, they will want you to sign a document called an NDA (Non-Disclosure Agreement). This is required because you are being exposed to some confidential and sensitive financial information about a business. Once you sign the NDA, you are in a contract that says you are not to disclose the information you are about to receive with just anyone.

Also, another thing to keep in mind when visiting any of the potential stores for sale, that most times the business owners do not want the employees to know that they are selling the business. Sometimes there is a good reason for it. So first sit down and figure out what your budget is, what your game plan is, and how soon you want to get into a business. Once you know these three, you are halfway there.

Just remember when you contact a business broker, they may ask you a lot of questions to figure out what, exactly, you are looking for. They may ask about your budget; it is usually a good idea not to answer that with a dollar figure, instead tell them that it varies depending on what is out there. This way they will show you a wide range of businesses. Some may be over your budget, and some below, but this way you can see where the market stands. It gives you a baseline of the highs and the lows of your market.

Once you have a list of 3-4 businesses to look at that is when your real work starts. First, you need to visit all the locations, so you have a visual feel for them. Take plenty of notes; best is to take notes where you write down the good the bad on each side so later you can see what the good points are and what the bad points are of a business and if the bad ones outweigh the good ones.

You can also use a marketing tool I often use called an MA-CP grid, where you draw a square box with 4 mini squares that are equal to the square in that big box and, on the left of this box, I write MA, which stands for Market Attractiveness and on the bottom I write CP or Competitive Positioning. I try to place each of the laundromats in one of those squares based on their location, sales, nearest competitors, etc.

If a laundromat has very high market attractiveness, you should place it on the high side of the quadrant.

Similarly, if a store has a very good competitive position in the market, it should be placed on the "high" side as well. Ideally, you want to pick the store/business that ranks high on both market attractiveness and competitive positioning. This way you know you are looking at a winner.

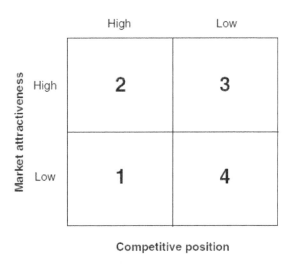

Once you narrow down to, let's say, 1-2 laundromats out the 5, time to tell your broker or seller that you are interested in finding out more about their business.

If you have come this far, then you are well on your way to be a business owner soon. But before you say yes, remember, once you narrow down to a handful laundromats, time to do a thorough due diligence on each of your findings.

Once you do good and thorough work, the right one will come out of that bunch, and you will know which business is the right one for you to make an offer on.

START-UP COST FOR BUILDING A LAUNDROMAT

A lot of new businesses fold because the owner does not set aside enough capital. To avoid this potential failure, you want a good laundry business plan with realistic targets as well as a revenue model of the best, the likely, and the worst outcomes. Also, have a few steps in place to increase business. Do not buy a Laundromat business solely on a seller's expected returns.

You also want to anticipate all upcoming expenses. Keep in mind that once you close escrow, you will need to stock a change machine(s) and pay a deposit for utilities. It is a good idea to have three to six months of expenses in a cash reserve. If you are building a brand new Laundromat business and obtaining all its equipment, you want to have a year of cash reserve set aside.

Do Not Do It Alone

Most new owners will try to reduce expenses in order to increase profits, and especially if they dread the tasks at hand as explained before, they should not do this. Most cut payroll and maintenance because they feel they can do such themselves, despite their inability to do a payroll or their lack of expertise in maintenance.

But, finally, most fail to see the tradeoff is time, besides affecting their mental health. Simply, when you hire the right help, you free up your time to focus on more important things, the things you are good at, such as marketing and expansion or the creative aspects of the business.

ESTIMATED COST TO OPEN ONE

Opening a laundromat business involves dealing with various governmental agencies for licenses and permits, just like any other business, if you follow the steps properly you can get it done in a reasonable amount of time. Opening a laundromat business successfully depends greatly on your access to some investment capital, also known as money.

It takes money to make money, and you are going to need access to money to open a laundromat business. Looking into whether or not you qualify for a business loan should be an option that you seriously consider if you can qualify for such.

There is no one-size-fits-all calculation that can estimate how much it will cost you to open a laundromat business. However, how much you will ultimately pay to open or buy a laundromat depends upon a number of factors that depend heavily on where you live, exactly where you plan to open your laundromat business, what kind of machines you are planning to install along with what other services you will be offering to your customers.

If you live in a moderate sized, non-metropolitan city, it might cost you $75,000 to $150,000 to open a laundromat business. However, if you live in a big metropolitan city, with a large inhabitant population and lots of customer traffic potential, then you might have to pay anywhere from $250,000 up to 1 million dollars to successfully open a laundromat business. Paying more than a million dollars is even potentially possible, depending on the situation.

The listing price for a laundromat business in Tampa, Florida can run about $495,000. On the other hand, a coin laundry I found in Benton Oregon for $85,000 only.

Check out this link to find laundromats for sale in the US

http://www.planetlaundry.com/industry-resources/stores-for-sale

EXPENSES TO BUILD A LAUNDROMAT

The first thing you will need, most obviously, is a building or a large room in a building. The *average*

Laundromat is about 2,000-3,000 square feet, and the *average* rent is about $2,000 -$6,000 a month. In a space this size, you can fit about 20 to 30 each of washers and clothes dryers. The biggest expense you will ever put into a Laundromat business is the cost of the washers and clothes dryers, owning or leasing them.

Yes, you will give thought later or next or alongside to things like offering vending machines, Wi-Fi, a television (or more than one) and the more creative offerings that will make your business unique and possibly a meeting place or just a preferred Laundromat, like a "food counter" where servers offer fresh sandwiches, etc. Or you may install video games, a kids play area, and etc. Basically, the creative aspects to choose from, if you so desire, for your Laundromat can be endless and exciting, depending on your goals and interests and creativity.

If you buy your equipment, not lease them, you can expect average washers and dryers to cost an average of $800-$1800 depending on their brand and condition (when buying used). If you invest in coin-operated machines, it is recommended you have a "change maker" machine available and well maintained. There is nothing like the turnoff of finding the "changemaker" broken or broken consistently or empty so that the consumer has to spend a lot of time tracking down those quarters that are hard to find and become rare when you most need them and that businesses are getting less and less likely to exchange paper money for.

Finally, banks, as we know, have "bank hours." They close early, they are barely open on weekends, and you cannot use the self-service machine at the bank to get quarters and change, and etc. So, really, after getting your equipment, your final cost is to set up your washers and clothes dryers, or have them set up, and any other machines, like that change maker or other creative aspects, like a food counter, if you are choosing such, to roll out when you first open your business or when you have a Grand Opening, and etc.

The cost of connecting your machines to the local sewer system will depend on the town or city you live in or the town or city you are choosing to set up your Laundromat business in. Sometimes the cost can be as high as $200 per washer. So, again, the cost can be higher or lower depending on your location. Based on these costs you are looking at about $20,000 in startup costs. With a decent credit score and some assets, you can get a loan, and your startup cost payment can be as low as about $400 a month. So the next question becomes whether or not you can turn a profit.

ESTIMATED COST OF OPENING A LAUNDROMAT IN A SMALL TO MID-SIZE CITY

ITEMS	COST
Lease Deposit, Insurance & License Fees	$3,500 - $50,000
Build out/Layout	$10,500 - $75,000
Equipment (New or gently used)	$50,000 - $135,000
Counter Top & Shelving	$1,000 - $3,000
Lighting & Signage	$2,000 - $10,000

POS, Credit Card & Video Equipment	$3,000 - $7,500
Food and Video Game Setup ***	$15,000-$50,000
Employee Training & Uniform	$1,500
Startup Cash	$5,000
TOTAL:	**$76,500 - $337,000**

*** Optional

ESTIMATED MONTHLY EXPENSES

Estimated Monthly Expenses	
Utility (Water, Gas, Elctrcity)	$3000 -$10,000
Rent	$2000 - $6000
Supplies (For Wash & Fold)	$500 -$750
Payroll (Attented Stores)	$3800-$8500
Maintenance & Repair	$1000-$3000
Insurance	$500 - $1000
Security Monitoring	$100-$500
Legal and Licenses	$100 - $250
Accounting/Bookkeeping	$75 - $150
Other Supplies	$150 - $200
Misc Expenses	$150-$350
Total Monthly Expenses	**$11,375 - $30,700**

ESTIMATED MONTHLY INCOME CALCULATION

Let's assume you have a laundromat with 15 Washers and 10 dryers. You also offer the "Wash and Fold" service along with a few video game consoles for the kids and a limited deli food options (Nachos, popcorns, soda, and coffee). In these type of laundromats, you also offer vending machines that offer laundry detergent and other similar products.

Based on industry statistics, a Laundromat washer is used about three to eight times a day costing the consumer an average of $3.00-$4.00 a load. Clothes dryers statistically bring in about 40 to 60 percent of the total of your Laundromat business revenue. So let us do some math.

Your Monthly Income: From the washing done by your consumers, you can expect to make an *average* of $6,750 (average 5 loads @ $3 per load per machine is $225 a day times 30 days). The clothes drying done by your consumers will produce an *average* of $4,050 (60 percent of the washer revenue). Let's also consider the "Wash and Fold" service which is typically priced at $1.25-$2.50 per pound. And in our case, let's assume you charge $1.75/lbs.

Let's look at the table below

Estimated Monthly Income

Revenue Washer	$6,750
Revenue Dryer	$4,050
Wash & Fold Service (100 lbs/day)	$4,500
Video Game Machine Revenue	$650
Income from Deli food	$1,500
Income from Vending	$850
Gross Monthly Income	**$18,300**

Not Net Income

Don't get excited seeing $18,300 in gross profit. It is gross profit and not NET PROFIT. You get net profit by deducting your expenses from your gross profit that is your "Take Home" money. That is the amount you make after paying everyone.

Take a look at this P&L (Profit & Loss) statement.

Jackie's Wash & Fold Laundromat
Profit and Loss Statement
December, 2016

Store Revenue:	Sales $		
Washer	6,750.00		
Dryer	4,050.00		
Wash & Fold	5,250.00		
Video Game Machine	650.00		
Deli Food Sales	2,500.00		
Vending Sales	1,250.00		
Cost of Goods Sold	750.00	Food and Vending Cost	
Gross Profit:		19,700.00	
Store Expenses:			
Payroll	3,950.00		
Utility	4,500.00		
Rent	2,750.00		
Insurance	650.00		
C.C. Charge	127.00		
Maintenance	780.00		
License &Mics	150.00		
Security	100.00		
Misc.	50.00		
Total Expense		13,057.00	
Net Profit:		6,643.00	

FIVE THINGS TO CHECK OUT BEFORE STARTING A LAUNDROMAT BUSINESS

With a little or a moderate amount of homework (or, even, a lot of homework, if you are that kind of person, who, like me, enjoys that homework, needs that homework, knowing it will give me a great foundation, as expressed before, and depending how you look at it, the time you spend being relative in a good way! ☺), a Laundromat business can be an excellent business opportunity for entrepreneurs.

Often, too, people choose to buy existing Laundromat businesses and their properties rather than starting new Laundromat businesses. Before you buy a Laundromat business though consider the following five things.

CHECK THE LEASE OF THE LAUNDROMAT BUSINESS

As I mentioned before, your lease is going to be one of your largest monthly expenses of your Laundromat business. This makes it one of the things that can make or break your Laundromat business. With a Laundromat business, you cannot simply move your Laundromat business if the lease does not work out for you since the equipment, plumbing and wiring are unique for the property.

You want to make sure your lease is long enough to allow you to recoup your investment or, in other words, that the lease is for at least an average of eight years. With a Laundromat business, be prepared to spend about 20 per cent of your gross revenue on the lease. The lease and/ or the details of it can cause you to garner one or several significant business risks.

WATER USE AND MANAGEMENT

Another big thing to consider when buying a Laundromat business is your water and/ or sewage costs. When buying an existing Laundromat business, look at the last two years of water usage and costs.

This not only tells you how much business the Laundromat business gets, how much traffic it gets, but it also sheds light on how efficient the equipment is. High numbers can also indicate a plumbing issue. If any of these elements alarm you, you need to explore and hunt down the whys. And possibly renegotiate or make financial plans to handle on your own or possibly look for another Laundromat business to buy.

LOCATION

I know I mentioned location a few times already, but I want to make sure you understand the importance of it. You should only buy a Laundromat business in an ideal location in order to have success. What does that mean? A Laundromat business needs to be close to customers, and it needs to be easy to access. The best Laundromat business is one located within a mile or two of apartment complexes so that you have a strong base, on paper, of regular customers.

Consider, though, that apartments, condos, and the like are more often now coming with washers and clothes dryers. So analyze the area apartments, etc., to see if this situation applies to your area when it did not years ago. Your location should also have plenty of parking, major road access, and nearby businesses, if your Laundromat business offers limited perks, to keep people busy while they wait. The best Laundromat business locations have three things:

1. Nearby apartment complexes (that more often than not do not come with washers and/ or clothes dryers).
2. Nearby universities and/ or other higher education campuses.
3. A busy shopping center with other businesses and no competitors.

In today's digital world, you also want to be aware of your Laundromat business' location in that consumers will compare its location online to others and decide which is better given their lifestyles and the ease of getting to the Laundromat businesses.

Plus, the overall look of your website, if you have one for your Laundromat business (and you probably should have one), should be pleasing and easy for consumers, potential customers, to navigate to find specific information, such as your hours of operation, how many washers and clothes dryers you have, whether or not your washers and clothes dryers operate with quarters and/ or with debit cards or credit cards, and, even, how your change machine operates, that is, whether you can operate it, too, with a debit and/ or credit card.

Again, people are going to search online when looking for a Laundromat business for this exact information, and your information concerning your Laundromat business should be readily available on your website if you choose to have a website, or on another website, if you choose to have it listed on another website.

Obviously having your own website for you Laundromat business is best and, if possible, it can even be better to have your own website *and* have it listed on another website.

EQUIPMENT

If the Laundromat business you purchase has old equipment, old washers, clothes dryers, and change machines, you can expect some big expenses right away. Before buying, be very sure to get make and model numbers for all the equipment such as washers, clothes dryers, and change machines. Front load washers and clothes dryers, on average, last about fifteen to twenty years, while top load washers last about seven to ten years.

If well maintained, they can last thirty and fifty years respectively. Any years beyond this and you can expect to replace them soon. Putting it delicately, customers tend to treat the machines of the Laundromat business less kindly than they would if they owned them or they came with their house, condo, dorm room, or apartment, and etc.

So before buying a Laundromat business make sure you thoroughly examine all the washer, clothes dryers and other machines and equipment. So not only having acquired as many manuals as needed (as discussed before), you should read your manuals and research, or at least familiarize yourself with how your research is laid out and same for the manuals so that if or when things break down, you have a place to begin, and, for those of you who panic, you will be less likely to do so, panic.

You can even call, "chat" with, or email the customer service department of your brand of machines with any questions or concerns you might have. You can also look into getting a professional to do the inspections for you. So ask yourself the following questions:

- Are the machines commercial grade?
- Are the machines clean?
- How old are the machines?
- Are there any current problems or maintenance issues with the machines?
- Are the machines coin operated, or digital, or both?

When assessing equipment, be sure to look for the following:

- Is there noticeably any broken equipment?
- Is there any visible damage on any of the machines?
- Are there any leaks coming from the washers?
- Is the equipment old and/ or worn out?
- Are there any failures in any of the drain systems?
- Are there any failures in the agitation mechanisms of the washers?
- Are there any issues with any of the coin slot mechanisms of any of the machines?
- Are there any issues with digital displays or card readers on your machines, if the machines have those instead of coin slots?*

*Do a few loads of your own laundry at all times of the day (or night if the Laundromat is open), and you will find out a lot concerning the above potential issues.

COMPETITION

You should also check out nearby Laundromat businesses to see what your competition is like. Ask yourself the following questions when considering your potential competition:

- Is (or are) the competitor laundry business (es) within two miles of your potential laundry business?
- Is there more than one Laundromat business within two miles of your Laundromat business?
- Do the other Laundromat businesses have a loyal customer base?
- What is the demographic of your competition?
- What are the hours of your competition?
- Do they offer other services?

　*And, again, do a few loads of laundry, perhaps, at your competitors' Laundromat businesses to see if there are any issues and to get a sense of the customers' satisfaction.

More often than not, if there are successful Laundromat businesses nearby, you should look elsewhere. But perhaps you can consider opening your Laundromat business where you had planned or hoped despite nearby competition if you are sure your amenities or approach will draw in other customers whose needs are different or you believe you will simply draw them in by what you offer.

But you more than likely should be sure those potential customers are around.

ADDITIONAL REVENUE STREAMS

Regardless of the location, look for opportunities to have products that can not only draw in customers but bring in extra revenue, such as:

- Wash & Fold service
- Vending machines
- Video game consoles
- Snack food, supplies

- Laundry supplies

Here, you already have five things to consider offering. Keep in mind, however, some of these products or services may require an attendant, except for, perhaps, a machine with laundry supplies or video games, or, even, old-fashioned pinball machines (another fun draw), and the upkeep of various services and the selling of certain products will be an additional service to have to monitor.

7 MOST IMPORTANT FACTORS TO CONSIDER WHEN LEASING A FACILITY

COMMERCIAL LEASE AGREEMENT

Date (For reference only): _____

1. **PROPERTY:** Landlord rents to Tenant and Tenant rents from Landlord, the real property and improvements _____ comprise approximately _____ % of the total square footage of rentable space in the entire property. description of the Premises.
2. **TERM:** The term begins on (date) _____
   (Check A or B):
   - ☐ A. **Lease:** and shall terminate on (date) _____ at _____ term of this agreement expires, with Landlord's consent, shall create a month-to-month tenancy that paragraph 2B. Rent shall be at a rate equal to the rent for the immediately preceding month, conditions of this agreement shall remain in full force and effect.
   - ☐ B. **Month-to-month:** and continues as a month-to-month tenancy. Either party may terminate the tenancy least 30 days prior to the intended termination date, subject to any applicable laws. Such notice may be
   - ☐ C. **RENEWAL OR EXTENSION TERMS:** See attached addendum _____
3. **BASE RENT:**
   A. Tenant agrees to pay Base Rent at the rate of (CHECK ONE ONLY:)
   - ☐ (1) $ _____ per month, for the term of the agreement.
   - ☐ (2) $ _____ per month, for the first 12 months of the agreement. Commencing with each 12 months thereafter, rent shall be adjusted according to any increase in the U.S. Consumer

DEMOGRAPHIC

It is important to consider foot traffic during the process of picking a location for your new laundromat. However, keep in mind you can have a large amount of foot traffic around or behind the store where they are not actually seeing you or passing your store where they can see your storefront.

However, to know whether or not this foot traffic will be in your target market is such an important step when you open a laundromat and it can have a considerable influence on your location choice. Think about where this foot traffic is coming from.

Think about their circumstance that they may be in that would make them want to purchase your coffee? It could be work, school, or college in the mornings, or perhaps home after having dinner, or going to an event near your business. Understanding your customer can help you better understand the goals of your business.

No matter how great the location seems, the better choice would be to open your laundromat near businesses or an office park. Remember that when you choose your location, it will always affect your profitability either adversely or positively based on how smart you are when picking the location, your goal is always to make choices that will impact your profitability positively.

As I mentioned earlier, doing a thorough analysis of each proposed location is very vital. It is not only essential, but it is also beneficial to think about more out of the box competitors. These would be anyplace that would allow your targeted customers to get what you provide.

Look at places such as dry cleaners and other laundromats or even wash and fold places. These businesses are in similar markets; they are all basically competing with the products you have.

Think about what are businesses are around your laundromat; sometimes some of these companies can help you by actually complementing your offerings. Having your laundromat near other businesses or a university could encourage students and employees to come to you first because of the added convenience of your location.

If you are near a mall or shopping center, you could receive traffic from those looking for a midday caffeine bump, while walking around and shopping.

ACCESSIBILITY

While customers will come back if the quality of your product offerings is good, if you are convenient, they are more likely to give you a try. Think about what your customer needs.

If they're driving cars, you have to provide convenient parking. For customers walking to or from various other locations, it is critical to be clearly visible from the street, without street accessibility, you could lose your customers to your competitors.

BUILDING INFRASTRUCTURE

Many times laundromats need a specific kind of building infrastructure. It is important to understand that not all spaces will be able to accommodate a laundromat type outlet. In most situations, you are looking for a cozy and comfortable space that fits the average number of customers you plan on having without feeling too crowded.

You also need to remember to make sure that the place has adequate plumbing, electrical and other utilities that are required to establish a laundromat. Also, you need to make sure there is room to set up the laundromat equipment in an efficient way, so your customers have adequate space to move around.

Another thing to consider besides the actual space is licensure. Some spaces don't allow certain businesses on their property. Make sure that you have inquired about this when you are choosing locations for your shop. You might want to check with your local city or county business licensing office to see if there are any such restrictions.

TERMS OF THE LEASE

When thinking of all the questions you will have to consider, the most obvious question that is often thought about when you are looking for the right location is "Can I afford it?" and "Can my customers afford it?"

If you choose a location with high rent costs, that cost will be transferred to your customers. While that isn't necessarily a bad thing, you have to keep the targeted customer in mind while making sure your prices are in line with your competitors.

You also need to think about whether a location needs any renovations. Small business loans are used to help cover building costs if you feel that renovations will leave you financially strained. Because it is a very big decision.

Most business owners will worry about taking out a business loan. When considering loan offers, there are quite a few things to check out. These things can include the total payback amount, ease of payback, and the lender's reputation. More on that little later.

After the cost of your building, there are a few lease terms you to be aware of that would help you figure out the best location for your shop. Here are some examples of these:

LENGTH OF THE LEASE

Remember that commercial leases are real, legally binding contracts. You are generally unable to easily break or change any of the terms. Talk to a lawyer, and get a full understanding before signing any agreements.

Read your lease and make sure you know if the landlord will be allowed to increase your rent after the lease is signed. Also, know the Insurance requirements. Different leases can require you to have a specific kind of insurance coverages that could increase your overall budget.

SECURITY DEPOSIT

Make sure that you know conditions for your security deposit return. It is essential to understand how much you will have to pay upfront and the exact process of getting that security deposit back. It is important to know who is responsible for maintaining the space and who is responsible for the costs.

NEGOTIATING THE LAUNDROMAT LEASE

You have to know what you want: In lease negation, your goal is to create a situation where everyone leaves feeling as they have won. It is your responsibility to know what you want and consistently pursue it.

Your potential landlord is looking out for their best interest, and you should know as well. If something is important to you, make sure to have it in writing. A verbal agreement won't be enough.

Your lease can be very limiting if you allow it to be. Make sure that what want is actually located somewhere in the language of your lease. Rank what you want in in three

1. Must Haves
2. Negotiable
3. Reaches

Remember that if you don't ask for it, you absolutely won't get it.

Understand what your potential landlord wants: Listen to what their goals entail, and then modify your negotiations to meet their needs as well. Make sure to listen to what they are giving in too, and what they are fighting for. Remember that absolutely everything is negotiable, but show some discretion and restraint when considering what know what to negotiate, and it's not always money.

Sometimes the rent just can't be changed, but CAM, construction cost and other building costs might be able to be negotiated.

Strive to find your best middle ground. Negotiating is all give and take. State what you want, and the reasons you want it.

Then tell them why it is essential to your business's success and then listen to their point of view as well. Then give up what you really don't need, for what they feel is very important.

HOW TO FINANCE A LAUNDROMAT BUSINESS

Once you have decided to purchase or start a Laundromat business, you are going to need to find a way to pay for it. There are a lot of factors that go into determining the financing for a Laundromat business, including the terms of financing, how much cash you have on hand, and how much cash flow you want to retain each month. For most, it is best to finance the business and if this is the case you have a few options.

Owner/Seller Financing

The best way to get financing for a used Laundromat business is to have the seller hold a note for some or all of the purchase amount. For the seller, there can be some tax advantages to receiving payments for the Laundromat business over time rather than all at once. A seller may also be open to the idea since they will still receive a steady income without having to run the business. This provides you with peace of mind since you can ensure the Laundromat business is really performing at the numbers the seller was claiming.

Home Equity Line of Credit (HELOC)

If you own a home, you may find yourself with a substantial amount of equity in your home and/ or a rental property you may own. If this is the case, then you might want to use that equity to buy a Laundromat business that gives you a monthly cash flow. When you use your equity to buy a Laundromat business, you are basically investing your equity.

Home Equity Lines of Credit (HELOC) loans also tend to have a lower interest rate than traditional business loans. In addition, Home Equity Lines of Credit (HELOC) loans are easier to qualify for and help to maximize your net cash flow to increase your overall return on your investment.

SMALL BUSINESS ADMINISTRATION LOANS (SBA)

For most businesses, the common loan is the Small Business Administration Loan (SBA). The Small Business Administration Loan is a full documentation loan. You will often need two to three years of personal income tax returns and a primary residence as collateral. The lender is also going to want to see two years of financial records of the Laundromat business you are looking to purchase plus the seller's tax returns.

If the Laundromat business has a declining revenue in the last two years, there is a good chance the loan will get denied, or you will be required to pay a higher down payment. However, with these SBA loans you typically only have to put down about 20 percent with interest rates around 1.5 to 3 percent above the prime rate based on your credit score. The downside is that these loans can take 45 to 60 days to close, so you will need a long escrow period in order to accommodate the lengthy funding process.

Before you determine which financing option is right for you, it is important to take the time to learn a little about financing and how it works.

OTHER FINANCING OPTIONS

When it comes to financing a new laundry business, it can be done through traditional financing or through equipment leasing. Since a Laundromat business will have a substantial amount of equipment, leasing companies can get around the issues of a new Laundromat business by using the equipment inside as collateral.

However, be careful when going this route as you do not want to end up with a large amount of money due at the end of the lease in order to purchase the Laundromat business or have a leasing company determine the amount due for your Laundromat business. Rather, make sure you are getting a finance lease that has a minimal amount purchase option at the end and have it in writing up front.

There are three steps of financing that you will need.

1. **Seed Capital**

   This is money for start-up, preparing your laundromat for opening followed by operating costs for a period of time before profits are made.

2. **Growth Capital**

   Funds to grow your business once you have proven it is a feasible concept and you are up and running.

3. **Harvest Cash**

   This is cash needed for when a partner, investor, or an owner wants their money out of the laundromat.

You have all this information built into your business plan. You need to have money for any of the above events six to nine months before it's needed.

Your seed capital or start-up is what you need to open. What are you going to put in your business plan? $80,000, $550,000, a million? Once you have determined what you need, don't undersell yourself. You may think asking for less will make it easier to get approved. Don't risk it.

Also, your banker or investor will need to see the use of these funds outlined in your business plan. For instance, do you need it all at once? Can a percentage be available but not drawn on until another stage?

For instance, your growth capital stage. These funds will be needed when you require a cash injection to continue growth to the point of stable profit-making.

You will also need a line of credit. Here's how that works. You project $80,000 in sales per month and want to have a two-month safety net of $160,000 cash. This is funding you will need to get from your banker as a line of credit. It serves as a safety net for start-ups.

The first source of capital is often the laundromat owner's own resources. Mortgages, IRAs, etc. After personal assets, an Angel Investor is the most common source of funds.

An Angel Investor is a private investor that will want a business plan, objectives, goals, strategy and projections before meeting with you.

They will also more than likely want a stake in your laundromat in exchange for their investment. Angel investors are the largest source of capital in the U.S. You can find them in investment clubs, and venture capitalist groups. Their trade group is called the Angel Capital Association.

You always have the option of funding via a partnership. However, at this point in the game, you would have already set-up the legal structure of your business and have resolved any investment issues with a partner.

Next, are banks, who are not always favorable towards start-ups. They get more interested when you need growth infusions of cash, buy-outs, and lines of credit because you have already proven yourself.

Banks do, however, have guidelines on how they will may approve your loan.

First is your character. Are you respected and well known? Can you pay the monthly loan payment? Your laundromat and equipment will be collateral but what else do you have?
How is your credit? Is your business plan clear, concise and feasible? Have you included realistic cash flow projections? Do you have the research and data to back-up what you are selling to them?

A banker wants to see a well-thought-out business plan, written by you, using your business experience and skills. Bankers are not crazy about plans for your laundromat that someone else has written.

That doesn't mean not getting the professional help you may need. What it means is that you better know your plan inside and out, can prove it and prove yourself to be capable.

Another funding alternative is the commercial finance companies. They typically have high-interest rates but are more likely to finance your start-up. In return, your interest rate will be anywhere from three to seven percent above prime.

The Small Business Administration (SBA) works with commercial lenders and will guarantee a loan up to 90%. They do, however, consider laundromats a substantial risk.
Again, a lot rides on your experience, skill, business acumen and a complete business plan when talking with the SBA.

Research who you will get a loan from as carefully as you have researched the rest of your dream

First, come up with a list of banks you want to apply to. It is not a good idea to apply at multiple banks at once. Instead, come up with a list of say, four banks, go and talk in depth with their business loan department and find out their full requirements.

In my experience, I have noticed typically smaller local banks are more inclined to offer loans to local small businesses such as restaurants, gas stations, and laundromats than some of the bigger banks. But that may not be true for every part of the country, so it is best to talk to at least 3-4 banks and try to get the feel if they are really into this sort of business financing or not before you submit your application.

Sometimes your local business brokers or commercial real estate agents can guide you to the right bank, as they often deal with similar situations and know which banks are more favorable to these sort of loans. You can also ask your bank that you deal with every day and ask their advice.

Once you narrow down to 2 banks, make trips to meet their loan officer and see what their requirements are. Just remember, every bank will have similar requirements, but they can still vary widely based on many factors, like how much down payment they require and how much collateral they need from you, even if they offer some SBA assisted loans or not. Your goal would be to deal with a bank that offers SBA loans.

SBA stands for Small Business Administration. SBA is a federal government agency whose primary goal is to help small business owners get financing.

Here is SBA website where you can read about their newest small business loan programs.
www.SBA.Gov

Most times the SBA offers some sort of guarantee (50-80%) on your behalf to the bank, so banks are somewhat more lenient in approving the loan as they are not in the risk for the total amount they are giving you. But the downside to this is the amount of paperwork you have to furnish is monumental in most cases.

The SBA's requirements can be broad and extensive, so be prepared to gather up a lot of paperwork.

Another drawback to an SBA loan is it can take up to 6 months to get approval from them. They run slower than most banks and, in their defense, they do have a lot of applicants that are submitting applications, so they have to go through all that, and it is always first come first served, so be patient.

But if you have a larger down payment (say 30% or higher) or have some good collateral to offer then you can opt out on SBA loans and get most any banks to offer you a conventional loan. Provided you have all your ducks in a row like your credit is in excellent shape, your tax returns show good incomes for previous years and so on so forth.

When you talk to any banks, they will hand you something called a loan package. Most times the package will have a checklist of documents that they want you to furnish to them along with a loan application and some other waiver forms, depending on your bank.

One thing to keep in mind: all banks and commercial lenders do have to follow certain guidelines that are set by federal and state banking authorities. Also, every bank will look at something called the LTV (Loan to Value) ratio of the property or business you are looking to buy. LTV is essentially where banks look at the actual value of the business you are looking to buy and how much of that value they can loan you.

But in any case, let's look at the list of documents you will need to get ready to submit to your bank. Some of these items I will mention here may not be on your bank's checklist but do gather them anyway as it will make you look more professional and business-like.

DOCUMENTS YOU WILL NEED FROM THE SELLER

- Last two years of P&L
- Last three years Tax Returns of the business
- A balance sheet
- Any and all health and equipment inspection reports and repair estimates

DOCUMENTS YOU WILL NEED FOR LOAN APPLICATION

1. You need to get copies of at least last 3 years of tax returns. Make sure the copies are signed.

2. Your resume (they may not even ask you for it, but remember the person that may approve your loan may never meet you but this way at least he or she gets to see who you are and how qualified you are. It always helps)

3. Copy of your Corp. Articles, (yes, you have to get this done before you even apply for your loan.)

4. Personal financial statement for all Corp. Officers or members. Make sure to sign it. If you are married and file joint tax returns than your wife needs to have one prepared for her as well, or you can make a joint personal financial statement for both of you and make sure you both sign that document.

5. Copy of the commercial appraisal (if applicable)

6. Copy of signed purchase agreement and Letter of Intent (if buying an existing laundromat)

7. Copy of your EIN (Employer's Identification Number) issued by the IRS

8. Copy of all member/partner's Driver's licenses and social security cards

9. A well thought out and expertly written Business Plan (not a store bought one or copy-pasted one; one that is written for that specific business. Get help if you need to, but this has to be a well thought out plan. Do it as your life depends on it. Trust me on this.)

10. Last but not least, the loan application all filled out. Use a computer and printer if possible. If not, write very clearly, so it is easy to read.

11. A cover letter addressed to the loan Dept. where you describe what is in the package and thanking them for reviewing your loan application. Lastly, tell them where they can find you if they need further help or additional documents from you. It just makes you look more professional

Now, remember to organize these papers with nice tabs and in a binding folder where anyone can open the folder, look at the tab and go directly to that specific section.

If you are applying for an SBA-specific business loan, then SBA may also give you a loan package with some more documents and forms to fill out.

Once the bank gives you the green light that your loan is approved, you need to ask them for a loan summery report. This will explain to you all the terms of the loan.

This is when you want to consider a fixed rate versus floating financing. Floating rates are always lower upfront, but have the potential to rise with prime rate fluctuations. Typically, accountants will arrange for a short-term loan with floating financing and a long-term loan with a fixed rate; but the ultimate choice is yours. With fixed-rate financing, you have a guaranteed monthly payment for the life of the loan, and you will not face any surprises no matter what the economy does.

Lenders prefer floating loans since it protects them. Banks will often borrow their money as floating loans and then charge more for a fixed rate loan so they can reduce their risks. When you ask about rates, the fixed rate is always going to be higher.

Once your Laundromat business location qualifies you with a lender, you will need to provide some necessary information and invest some money of your own. Most lending institutions want to see an investment of 20 to 30 percent. This investment needs to be for the entire project, including the equipment, the installation, and the leasehold improvements.

Plus, you will want additional cash on hand for startup costs, such as the utility deposits, the initial advertising, and a reserve to carry you until you reach the breakeven point.

PLANNING & BUILD-OUT

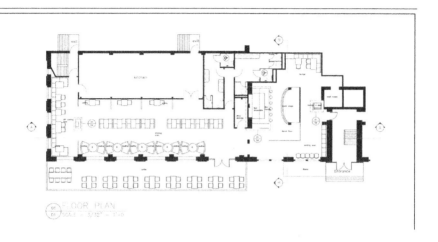

PLANNING STAGE

As I mentioned earlier, depending on your city, county and state's requirements, and the location you are trying to lease, you may be required to submit some type of plans of what you are trying to accomplish.

It could be as little as a simple hand-drawn plan for your local county plumbing and building department showing what and how you will lay out all your laundromat equipment. If you are planning on installing a certain type of cooking equipment such as a commercial fryer or a grill, then you may be required to install a commercial ventilation hood system. So be aware of that as it can get very expensive very fast.

Your best bet would be to first think about what food item you want to sell at your location along with snacks, soft drinks, and coffee. My advice is not to get into a grill or fryer as they do require so much more changes to an existing building.

In the event, if you need a total makeover, meaning you are asked to rebuild a whole interior of a building (total build-out), you will need to hire an architect to get a set of plans drawn. But for this to happen, you will need to furnish specific information to your architect.

1. How many machines you want in the facility
2. A list of all equipment you will be using along with their specs so an electrical design can be drawn based on the actual load.
3. How many restrooms you will need
4. What type of lighting fixtures you prefer to install

5. If you will have any cooking equipment, food warmer or any other food related equipment in the facility
6. All plumbing requirements according to the plumbing and health department code (if you will need a three compartment sink, a mop sick, etc.)
7. A layout of your counters and checkout stand
8. Exact area of placement for all your vending machines

Once you provide such information, the architect will then start drawing up the all the plans along with an HVAC plan based on the current city or county code.

Once they are done with the plan, they will send it off to your city or county building inspector for proper approval. Once the set of plans are approved, then your work will start.

Time for you to either hire a general contractor or if it is allowed in your city, you can act as the general contractor and hire sub-contractors to finish various jobs that need to be done according to the plan.

For example, you can hire a licensed plumber to do all the plumbing work, hire an HVAC company to get all your AC related work done and so on.

Last time I had to get a full set of plans for a full-blown laundromat (with kid's area, food, and gaming), it cost me around $6,000, but that was a full set of plans which included everything from wall décor to HVAC and everything in between.

Before you get all nervous, let me assure you, if you are just opening a basic laundromat, chances are you won't have to do all that. But I wanted to mention this because in certain city or state all these may be requirements based on what you are renting.

It may not be a bad idea to discuss your goal and plans with the city or county building and plumbing inspectors to get an idea of what might be involved this way you will be better prepared for what will come next.

BUILD-OUT

This is a stage where you see your laundromat coming to life little by little. Whatever you envisioned it to be, you will now see it coming together piece by piece.

Regardless if you hired a general contractor or an interior designer, but this is the stage where things will happen fast. So make sure to have all your ducks in a row.

Make sure to install/place all your big equipment before installing the counter tops, this way you won't have any gaps or holes. Get any and all HVAC, plumbing and electrical work done.

Test out all your electrical components to make sure everything is in working condition. Once that is done, time to start painting the walls. Hang all the decors once you are done the painting.

But before you bring in the washers and dryers, time to start laying your floor tiles or vinyl planks, whichever you picked. Let the floor settle for a few days before bringing the equipment.

Once you are done with all this, time to call on your health and building inspector for their final inspection so you can get the CO (certificate of occupancy) without which you can open your business.

BUYING LAUNDROMAT EQUIPMENT FOR YOUR LAUNDROMAT BUSINESS

You basically just need washers and clothes dryers, right? There is actually a little more to it. Perhaps the most important and essential part of buying or starting a Laundromat business is the purchase of and/ or renting of some or all of your equipment. After all, the machines are the backbone of your Laundromat business.

There are a few things you need to consider before buying equipment for your Laundromat business. Not all Laundromat business equipment is the same obviously so you need to know what you are looking for to ensure you are getting the best value for your money, as this is part of your business investment.

First, there are two types of washers. Most people think of conventional top-loading washers. Basically, the clothes go into a large "bucket" in the machine, that bucket that fills with water, also the bucket being where you put the soap, and then an agitator moves the clothes around in the "bucket" so they become clean. These types of washers are starting to be phased out and are being replaced by front load washers.

A front load washer does not have an agitator and relies on a tumbling action. These new front load washers also have a greater capacity, in that they can hold more clothes.

Second, when it comes to washers and clothes dryers, there are dozens of brand options. The four most common brands sold in the United States are:

- Maytag
- Speed Queen
- Dexter
- Wascomat

What you choose will depend on four things:

First, you are going to want to find equipment that is durable since you are going to need it to stand up to constant use. You do not want to wait for repairs every month or so since this can be an inconvenience for you and for the customers and cause them to go elsewhere.

Second, you are going to want to make sure you have high capacity equipment that will provide your customers with options. Remember, you are serving the customers without laundry facilities at home, those whose home washer and/ or clothes dryer is broken, as well as those who need larger washing machines for items they only wash occasionally, such as comforters, for example.

Third, you want to consider purchasing energy efficient equipment. But energy efficient, may, for now, be maintaining your present washers and dryers and other equipment until they cannot be fixed anymore or *truly* cost you more maintaining them than it would be buying new energy efficient washers and dryers, instead of tossing them off into a landfill.

This will not only help you to keep down the cost of your utilities and/ or replacements, but it will also show your customers that you care about the environment by reducing your energy usage and/ or concern for landfills and our disposal happy country and it will *actually* help the environment.

Lastly, you want to purchase equipment based on what you think, after research, will make your customers happy. If all else fails, consider what you would like to use if you were in their positions. This means you want equipment that is easy to use and with options so that doing laundry is both easy and meets a variety of needs.

It can also be a good idea to have equipment with their times needed to complete their tasks as short as possible while still providing good service to help customers manage their own time. If you are not going to have staff on hand at all times, it is especially important that your equipment be easy to use.

How & Where to Find good used Equipment

Here are few websites where they sell both new and used laundromat equipment. Take a look. But please know this that I am not an affiliate for any of these sites, so I am not recommending any of these sites, this is only for you to get an idea. Depending on when you read this, you may want to do a search on Google and see what else is available out there.

1. BDS Laundry Solution
https://www.bdslaundry.com/equipment_categories/closeout-laundry-equipment/

2. CSC Service Works
http://www.macgray.com/laundry_equipment/equipment_sales/

3. Coin Laundry Association

http://www.coinlaundry.org/openforumlink/community-home/digestviewer?communitykey=36be8a2a-828f-4590-a588-12b142cd5c3d&tab=digestviewer

4. eBay Stores

http://stores.ebay.com/123laundry/Used-Laundry-Equipment-/_i.html?_fsub=5029161

5. Superior Laundry Equipment

http://superior-laundry.com/

PERMITS & BUSINESS LICENSES (UNCLE SAM)

NAME YOUR BUSINESS

This is the first thing on the list for a number of reasons. First, branding will be critical to your business. You have to be able to stand out from the other shops near you; customers need to know why you are different, and superior to your competition in order to give your laundromat a chance. So now you need a great name that stands out.

Here are some things to consider. Your name must be relevant in some way to who you are, your business, or your location. It needs to be connected to what you do. Your name should be short enough to be easily remembered. When you choose your name, it has to be unique, meaning not being used by any other company.

Google the name you have chosen and see if another business pops up, if not you are in great shape. Checking your business name with the Patent and Trade Mark Office to ensure that it is unique is another sure-fire method. Once you find the unique name that you want, it is time to buy the domain for the name of your business.

For example, if you have named you laundromat "Jackie's Laundromat," you want to buy the domain "jackieslaundromat.com" you might want to buy other top-level domains or TDLs. Examples of other ones are ".net" or ".biz." buying these can prevent others from being able to use your name with these TDLs. Most domain sellers such as GoDaddy.com offer packages that allow you to purchase the domain with multiple TDLs.

INCORPORATING YOUR BUSINESS

Every business needs to have the proper license, permits and other authorizations to be able to perform its normal course of business. When you choose a legal entity for your used laundromat there are two main factors to consider:

- What you want
- The type of business model you intend to build

Often you have the option of choosing to file as a limited liability company or LLC, general partnership or even sole proprietorship. A sole proprietorship is the ideal business structure for someone starting a used laundromat, especially if it is a moderate start from your home. However, most prefer the benefits of an LLC.

If you plan to eventually expand your used laundromat to other locations or potentially online, then you definitely don't want to file as a sole proprietor. In this instance, you should definitely file as an LLC.

When you file as an LLC, you will be able to protect yourself from personal liability. This means that if anything goes wrong while operating your business then only the money you invested into the company is at risk.

This isn't the case if you file as a sole proprietor or a general partnership. LLCs are simple and flexible to operate since you won't need a board of directors, shareholder meetings or other managerial formalities in order to run your business.

Here are all the legal business structures you can choose from, it is best to get some advice from your CPA or accountant or an attorney.

LEGAL BUSINESS STRUCTURE

When starting a business, there are five different business structures you can choose from:

- Sole Proprietor

- Partnership

- Corporation (Inc. or Ltd.)

- S Corporation

- Limited Liability Company (LLC)

SOLE PROPRIETOR

This is not the safest structure for a laundromat. It is used for a business owned by a single person or a married couple. Under this structure, the owner is personally liable for all business debts and may file their personal income tax.

PARTNERSHIP

If your business is owned and operated by multiple people, when it comes to structuring your business, you can choose one of two kinds of partnerships. These two kinds of partnerships are general partnerships and limited partnerships.

In a general partnership, the partners manage the business together and are responsible for each other debts. A limited partnership actually has both limited and general partners.

The general partners work as previously described, but the limited partners are only investors that don't actually have any control over the company and are not responsible for the debts in the same way.

CORPORATION (INC. OR LTD.)

The corporate structure is complex and costs quite a bit more money than most other business structures. This is because a corporation is a completely independent legal entity. It is separate from its owners. It also requires you to comply with more regulations and requirements.

A corporation provides increased liability protection for the business owner or owners. A corporation's debt is not considered that of its owners. This lessens your personal risk.

It isn't a very common structure among laundromat since there are shares of stocks involved.

Profits are taxes both are at the corporate level and distributed to shareholders. When you structure a business at this level, there are often lawyers involved.

S CORPORATION

This is one of the most popular types of business entity people forms to it avoid double taxation. It is taxed similarly to a partnership entity. But an S Corp. needs to be approved to be classified as such, so it isn't very common among laundromats.

The S corporation is going to be a more attractive option for small-business owners than a regular corporation. That's because an S corporation takes some great parts of what a corporation offers on a smaller, less expensive scale. It has some very appealing tax benefits as well as provides business owners with the liability protection of a corporation.

You have a couple of choices when it comes to filing the necessary paperwork for your business. The first is to have a lawyer or accountant to file a legal business entity for you.

You can also do it yourself using online resources, or by going to your local city office and filling out the necessary paperwork. You can go on websites like leaglzoom.com and draw up the document for less money than what an attorney would charge you to do the same.

LIMITED LIABILITY COMPANY (LLC)

This is the most common business structure among laundromats. It offers benefits for small businesses since it reduces the risk of losing all your personal assets in case you are faced with a lawsuit. It provides a clear separation between business and personal assets. You can also elect to be taxed as a corporation, which saves you money come tax time.

If you are unsure which specific business structure you should choose then, you can discuss it with an accountant. They will direct you to the best possible option for what your business goals are. Just remember you should always get some sound legal advice when filing your corporation.

I filed my first LLC via Legalzoom.com as I didn't have the extra funds to hire an attorney. Thankfully it worked out well for me.

APPLY AND OBTAIN YOUR EMPLOYER IDENTIFICATION NUMBER FROM IRS

EIN or Employer Identification number is essentially social security or tax identification number but for your business. IRS and many other governmental agencies can identify your business via this unique nine-digit number.

Remember you will not need this number if you choose to be a sole proprietorship for your business.

It is simple to apply, either you can do it yourself or get your accountant to apply for you, but the process is simple, you fill out the form SS-4, which can be filed online, via Fax or via mail.

Here is a link to IRS website where you can download or fill out the form online.

https://www.irs.gov/businesses/small-businesses-self-employed/how-to-apply-for-an-ein

Form SS-4 — Application for Employer Identification Number

Form SS-4
(Rev. January 2010)
Department of the Treasury
Internal Revenue Service

Application for Employer Identification Number
(For use by employers, corporations, partnerships, trusts, estates, churches, government agencies, Indian tribal entities, certain individuals, and others.)
▶ See separate instructions for each line. ▶ Keep a copy for your records.

OMB No. 1545-0003
EIN

Type or print clearly.

1. Legal name of entity (or individual) for whom the EIN is being requested

2. Trade name of business (if different from name on line 1)
3. Executor, administrator, trustee, "care of" name

4a. Mailing address (room, apt., suite no. and street, or P.O. box)
5a. Street address (if different) (Do not enter a P.O. box)

4b. City, state, and ZIP code (if foreign, see instructions)
5b. City, state, and ZIP code (if foreign, see instructions)

6. County and state where principal business is located

7a. Name of responsible party
7b. SSN, ITIN, or EIN

8a. Is this application for a limited liability company (LLC) (or a foreign equivalent)? ☐ Yes ☐ No
8b. If 8a is "Yes," enter the number of LLC members ▶

8c. If 8a is "Yes," was the LLC organized in the United States? ☐ Yes ☐ No

9a. Type of entity (check only one box). Caution. If 8a is "Yes," see the instructions for the correct box to check.
☐ Sole proprietor (SSN) _____
☐ Partnership
☐ Corporation (enter form number to be filed) ▶
☐ Personal service corporation
☐ Church or church-controlled organization
☐ Other nonprofit organization (specify) ▶
☐ Other (specify) ▶
☐ Estate (SSN of decedent) _____
☐ Plan administrator (TIN)
☐ Trust (TIN of grantor)
☐ National Guard   ☐ State/local government
☐ Farmers' cooperative   ☐ Federal government/military
☐ REMIC   ☐ Indian tribal governments/enterprises
Group Exemption Number (GEN) if any ▶

9b. If a corporation, name the state or foreign country (if applicable) where incorporated
State | Foreign country

10. Reason for applying (check only one box)
☐ Started new business (specify type) ▶
☐ Hired employees (Check the box and see line 13.)
☐ Compliance with IRS withholding regulations
☐ Other (specify) ▶
☐ Banking purpose (specify purpose) ▶
☐ Changed type of organization (specify new type) ▶
☐ Purchased going business
☐ Created a trust (specify type) ▶
☐ Created a pension plan (specify type) ▶

11. Date business started or acquired (month, day, year). See instructions.
12. Closing month of accounting year
14. If you expect your employment tax liability to be $1,000 or less in a full calendar year and want to file Form 944 annually instead of Forms 941 quarterly, check here. (Your employment tax liability generally will be $1,000 or less if you expect to pay $4,000 or less in total wages.) If you do not check this box, you must file Form 941 for every quarter. ☐

13. Highest number of employees expected in the next 12 months (enter -0- if none). If no employees expected, skip line 14.
Agricultural | Household | Other

15. First date wages or annuities were paid (month, day, year). Note. If applicant is a withholding agent, enter date income will first be paid to nonresident alien (month, day, year) ▶

16. Check one box that best describes the principal activity of your business.
☐ Health care & social assistance ☐ Wholesale-agent/broker
☐ Construction ☐ Rental & leasing ☐ Transportation & warehousing ☐ Accommodation & food service ☐ Wholesale-other ☐ Retail
☐ Real estate ☐ Manufacturing ☐ Finance & insurance ☐ Other (specify) ▶

17. Indicate principal line of merchandise sold, specific construction work done, products produced, or services provided.

18. Has the applicant entity shown on line 1 ever applied for and received an EIN? ☐ Yes ☐ No
If "Yes," write previous EIN here ▶

Third Party Designee
Complete this section only if you want to authorize the named individual to receive the entity's EIN and answer questions about the completion of this form.
Designee's name | Designee's telephone number (include area code)
Address and ZIP code | Designee's fax number (include area code)

Under penalties of perjury, I declare that I have examined this application, and to the best of my knowledge and belief, it is true, correct, and complete.
Name and title (type or print clearly) ▶ | Applicant's telephone number (include area code)
 | Applicant's fax number (include area code)

OPENING A COMMERCIAL BANK ACCOUNT

This is one important step, but it can only be done after you have a fully executed article of incorporation which has been approved by the state, and you have an EIN number assigned by the IRS.

Once you have these two documents, you should be able to go to a bank and open your first commercial bank account.

But remember to check and understand various types of commercial checking account fees, you want to find a bank that offers free or almost free commercial checking account because some larger banks can charge you hundreds of dollars each month depending on how many transactions you do. Make sure to ask and shop around before you sign on the dotted line.

CITY & COUNTY LICENSES

Since you are opening a laundromat with some food service business, one of the most essential steps in your licensing process should be to discuss your proposed plan and operation with your local county health department. As they will be the ultimate authority to issue you a food permit without which you can operate your food(deli)business.

Next step would be to go to your local city and county business licensing office and find out what type of business and regulatory licenses you are required to have. It should take a few days to get your licenses and permits in place, and then you are finally and officially in business.

You also need to attend a 4-6 hour class to obtain your SafeServ permit. This is a certificate that ensures that the manager or the owner of any food-related businesses know how to handle food safely.

Each establishment needs to have minimum one person who is certified in the SafeServ program.

THREE WAYS TO INCREASE YOUR CUSTOMER FLOW

Once you own a Laundromat business, it can be easy to get caught up in the day-to-day activities of owning a Laundromat business, but you should take the time to find a way to increase your customer base. Studies have shown that the average return on the investment for a laundry business facility is 20 to 35 percent.

You can maintain a steady profit and even expand it by finding ways to grow your customer base. Here are three things you can do to increase your customer flow.

UPGRADED EQUIPMENT

Most commercial laundry equipment has a lifespan of 5 to 15 years. You should consider the previous discussion about the environment and your equipment, but, as discussed, choosing to upgrade your equipment not only benefits you as a Laundromat business owner, but it also increases your customer base. Newer equipment with newer technology provides customers with a unique and positive experience.

By replacing old equipment, considering, again, what was discussed previously about the environment, you possibly can be ensuring that your equipment is working at full potential and decreasing any downtime that can lead to unsatisfied customers. If you choose this route, you can also attract new customers by advertising your Laundromat business as having state of the art equipment.

ADDING TECHNOLOGY

One of the biggest priorities you should have is to provide a convenient experience for your customers, again, keeping in mind what has been discussed about environmental issues. The best way you can do this today is to add technology to your Laundromat business. There is a wide range of benefits you can get from adding technology to increase customers and also strengthen the loyalty of your existing customers. When you add technology, you are differentiating yourself from the standard coin-operated laundry business in four main ways:

1. You are offering customers a convenient way to pay with various methods.
2. Your equipment will have user-friendly displays and interfaces.
3. You can authorize payments in real time.
4. You can offer your customers options, such as machine availability and countdown options.

ADDING AMENITIES

One of the keys to success in the Laundromat business is differentiation. You always want to look for ways to enhance the experience of your customers. One way to do this is to add amenities to your Laundromat. Some options you can consider include the following:

- Laundry Carts
- Soap vendors
- Hanger vendors
- Bag vendors
- Bill changers

While these five areas are helpful for increasing your customer base, the fact is you still need a strong marketing plan to help advertise your Laundromat business concerning these areas.

LAUNDROMAT BUSINESS MARKETING STRATEGIES

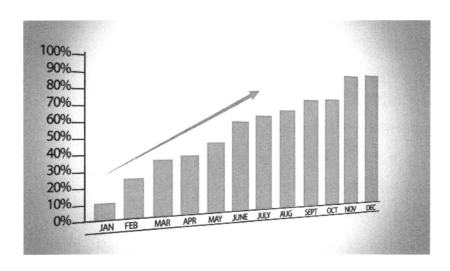

When it comes to marketing strategies for a Laundromat business, they often follow much of the same patterns as that of any other business but with a few different details. So let us take a look at how you can possibly develop a strategy for marketing your Laundromat business.

DETERMINING YOUR AUDIENCE

Before you create and start any marketing strategies, you want to determine your audience. To do this, you need to, mostly, locate those in your community who do not have their own washers and clothes dryers. Neighborhoods that have high concentrations of student housing or large rental zones are often right places.

Other places can be those with people who do not stay in place for long such as long-term hotels or corporate housing developments. You should also keep in mind offering your Laundromat business service to those who do not have the means to buy their own washers and clothes dryers, such as seniors and/ or low-income families and individuals.

ADVERTISE YOUR SERVICES

Most customers expect that at standard Laundromat businesses there will be washers and clothes dryers and folding stations. However, you want to attract a larger customer base by advertising what makes your Laundromat business different. Do you offer any of the following?

- Wi-Fi
- Television (s)
- Entertainment, such as video games

- Music
- Play area for children

If you have any of these or other amenities in your Laundromat business, then you want to advertise them with your marketing materials through all of the kinds of media you can handle. These, more often than not, can be deciding factors for customers choosing a Laundromat Business to go to.

MARKETING DISTRIBUTION

This is where those of you especially interested can allow your creativity to take over or bloom concerning your laundry business. So consider the number of places where you can advertise, such as through or with the following:

- Perhaps you can advertise with or offer materials about your laundry business to realtors so they can pass on the information to their clients.
- Perhaps you can post on rental associations' "boards."

- Sometimes it is possible to post within college media, such as in bulletins, within their digital media, and on their standard bulletin boards.
- Advertise in local laundromats and laundromats by posting nicely designed flyers on their community bulletin boards.
- Advertise at local grocery stores and movie theaters by placing beautifully designed flyers on their community boards or, as in the case of movie theaters, consider buying "space" to promote your business among other "film" advertisements, like those of other local businesses all shown before the movie starts.

It is also essential that you focus on the top three ways to market your Laundromat business.

TOP THREE WAYS TO MARKET YOUR LAUNDROMAT BUSINESS

Owning a Laundromat business puts you in a very competitive service industry so that you need to make smart and informed decisions to stand out from the competition. You can easily maintain your customer base by upgrading equipment, adding technology and reducing downtime, but what about getting new clients and being unique from the competition. There are three big things you need to or can do.

EXTERIOR SIGNS

As a Laundromat business owner, you are probably operating with a small budget. A cost-effective option is to use exterior signs to promote your laundry business. A study by the Coin Laundry Association (CLA) found that 60 percent of customers believe signs reflect the quality of services or products. Signs can range in price from a few hundred dollars to thousands of dollars; when choosing your sign, be sure to do, consider and/ or incorporate the following:

- Use bright and contrasting colors.
- Use bold fonts for easy reading.
- Keep in mind the color and architecture of your building.
- Read over the signed addendum on your lease.

LOCAL AREA/STORE MARKETING (LAM/LSM)

Most Laundromat businesses serve customers with a lower income. Those having a lower income often have to use their smartphones as their Internet unfortunately or, depending on who you ask, maybe as a positive in that their lives are freed in that they have one less distraction or contraption to maintain.

Regardless, this is why you need to focus on local marketing as a way to increase your visibility during their searches on their smartphones and so that those wielding only smartphones and those in need of a Laundromat business can find you.

GIVING BACK TO THE COMMUNITY

Lastly, it can be a good idea to be, for your laundry business to be, a partner with or a "sister" of a local charity or charities and similar organizations, since it will extend your local marketing and, more importantly, give back to the community that supports your laundry business and, simply, you.

I hope we have helped you continue to consider opening a Laundromat business, or, even, decide the Laundromat business is not for you, given all the information in this book. Either way, I consider both outcomes, the one you came to with our (there are two authors of this book — I'm just finishing it!), given our, words, the right one or the right one as yet to be!

LAST WORDS

I want to say THANK YOU for purchasing and reading this book. I really hope you got a lot out of it!

Can I ask you for a quick favor though?

If you enjoyed this book, I would really appreciate it if you could leave me a Review on Amazon.

I LOVE getting feedback from my wonderful readers, and reviews on Amazon really do make the difference. I read all of my reviews and would love to hear your thoughts.

Thank you so much!!

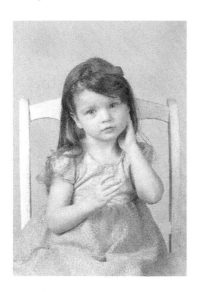

RESOURCES FOR LAUNDROMAT BUSINESS

www.americancoinop.com/articles/us-census-bureau-shines-light-laundromat-history

http://www.supersudslaundries.com/quick-history-laundromat/

www.theatlantic.com/business/archive/2017/07/decline-american-laundromat-gentrification/535257/

http://www.keewes.com/blog/history-of-laundromats

https://homesteady.com/info-10011491-rotary-washing-machine.html

https://www.hunker.com/13410374/the-history-of-the-clothes-dryer

www.google.com/search?source=hp&ei=KFtFWoa6JOLk_Q auzYuYDw&q=history+of+the+dryer&oq=history+of+the+dry er&gs_l=psy-ab.3..0i22i30k1l10.1557.5656.0.5929.21.17.0.3.3.0.159.115

4.16j1.17.0....0...1c.1.64.psy-ab..1.20.1174.0..0j0i131k1.0.EgD3Te4AV0E

http://www.washcycle.com/history-clothes-dryer/

https://topiclessbar.wordpress.com/2011/02/23/better-than-hanging-the-history-of-the-dryer/

http://www.washing-machine-wizard.com/washer-dryer-history.html

http://www.wweek.com/portland/article-22204-spin-laundry-lounge-quick-slosh.html

Dave & Busters 1/23 2/27
Creve Croeur 2/19
Fitz Lunchr 2/20
Arch Fun Day 2/12
Arch Fun Day 1/8